SMALL TRAGEDY

by

Craig Lucas

SAMUEL FRENCH, INC.

45 West 25th Street
NEW YORK 10010
LONDON

7623 Sunset Boulevard
HOLLYWOOD 90046
TORONTO

IMPORTANT BILLING AND CREDIT REQUIREMENTS

All producers of *SMALL TRAGEDY must* give credit to the Author of the Play in all programs distributed in connection with performances of the Play and in all instances in which the title of the Play appears for purposes of advertising, publicizing or otherwise exploiting the Play and/or a production. The name of the Author *must* appear on a separate line on which no other name appears, immediately following the title, and *must* appear in size of type not less than fifty percent the size of the title type.

In addition the following credit *must* appear in all programs distributed in connection with the Work:

Playwright's Horizons, Inc. New York City produced the New York Premiere of SMALL TRAGEDY Off-Broadway on February 17, 2004

SMALL TRAGEDY was developed and originally produced with the support from The Playwrights' Center McKnight Commission and Residency Program, Minneapolis, Minnesota.

SMALL TRAGEDY by Craig Lucas was originally co-produced by the Hidden Theatre and The Playwright's Center June 6th – 29th, 2003 in Minneapolis, Minnesota. The co-producer was Polly Carl, the production manager was Erica Christ and the stage manager was Angie Diermeier. The scenic designer was Erik Paulsen, costume design by Alicia C. Vegell, lighting design by Karin Olson, and sound design by C. Andrew Mayer. The composers were Chris Speed and Skuli Sverrisson. The production was directed by Kip Fagan. The cast was as follows:

Jen	ANNELISE CHRIST
Fanny	MAGGIE CHESTOVICH
Nate	VINCENT DELANEY
Hakija	BRENT DOYLE
Paola	AMY McDONALD
Christmas	PETER MIDDLECAMP

PLAYWRIGHTS HORIZONS

Tim Sanford
Artistic Director

Leslie Marcus
Managing Director

William Russo
General Manager

presents

SMALL TRAGEDY

A New Play by

CRAIG LUCAS

Featuring

Rob Campbell
Lee Pace

Rosemarie DeWitt
Ana Reeder

Daniel Eric Gold
Mary Shultz

Sets by
Douglas Stein

Costumes by
Marina Draghici

Lighting by
Jennifer Tipton

Sound by
John Gromada

Casting
James Calleri, C.S.A.

Director of Development
Jill Garland

Production Manager
Christopher Boll

Production Stage Manager
Thom Widmann

Directed by

MARK WING-DAVEY

ACT I

Scene 1

JEN. I still couldn't say whose tragedy this is, was. Hakija's? Fanny's, Chris', Paola's, Nate's? Mine. Or if it *is* a tragedy. Nate explained to us all once what constitutes tragedy and what is simply a very sad thing. He neglected to say whether a tragedy belongs to the participants, to those suffering, or to the people watching them suffer.

Scene 2

(Onstage, PAOLA, JEN, NATHANIEL. In the corridor, CHRISTMAS and HAKIJA.)

PAOLA .
This is Jennifer Helburn––   NATHANIEL.
brun–   Hi.
Nathaniel Townsende.
     JEN. Nice to meet you.
     NATHANIEL. You're readinnnnng – ?
     JEN & PAOLA. Jocasta.
     NATHANIEL. Anything you want to ask me?

JEN. No, I think it's pretty clear. You – ?

PAOLA. I'll read Oedipus.

JEN. Okay.

PAOLA.

"Jocasta, the man we sent for earlier, is that the man he means?"

JEN.

... Sorry.

NATHANIEL. Take your time.

PAOLA. I'll give it to you again:

"Jocasta, the man we sent for earlier, is that the man he means?"

JEN.

"What man? Who cares what he means? Why even ask, forget it, it's not worth knowing."

PAOLA.

"What? I can't stop now when I'm about to see the truth of my birth!"

JEN.

"By the gods, I beg you stop! If you love your own life, stop, I've been tortured enough, haven't I?"

PAOLA.

"You stop! Even if I'm discovered to be the child of slaves, you're not disgraced!"

JEN.

"Please, do what I say, don't ask why!"

PAOLA.

"You'll never stop me from finding out the truth."

JEN.

"I want what is best for you."

PAOLA.

"That is the very thing that's tormenting me."

JEN.

"God help you, Oedipus, and keep the truth away from you.
Secrets should be kept."

PAOLA.

"Someone go find the shepherd, let my wife take pride in her
nobility."

JEN.

"Goodbye, my poor deluded, lost, cursed, those are the last
names I'll ever give you."

NATHANIEL. Good. Very good. Nice.

JEN. Thanks.

NATHANIEL. Thanks. Very much.

JEN. It's been a long time since I've auditioned.

NATHANIEL. No, that was wonderful, thank you.

JEN. Weren't–? I think I missed you at Yale by one year.

NATHANIEL. Oh. Yeah? Are you Equity?

JEN. No, long story. I – I'm just finally getting back to it.

NATHANIEL. Well, thank you.

JEN. Can I do another speech?

NATHANIEL.

Well,	PAOLA.
we're on a tight –	I think –

JEN. Please? I'll be quick.

NATHANIEL. Sure. (To *PAOLA.*) It's okay. You're great.
I love you.

JEN.

This is the Messenger, right after ... Well ...

"Jocasta's dead: her own hand.

You weren't there, you can't know how horrible it was.

I was. I was there. She burst in, our Queen,

Now demented and wringing her hair,

Running through doors, running, then locks herself in the

bedroom, crying:
"Laius! Here is our bed! Soiled.
Filthy *soil* bringing forth a husband by a husband,
And children by a child! All soiled.
We made love!" ... Which we does she mean?
...
We move–But then the son, husband, King, Prince, raving,
stamping up and down; bellows:
"A weapon! Now! Where is she? Find me that double
breeding ground!, Where?"
And hurls himself against the door, again, breaking the bolts,
falling to his knees before: ... wife ... mother ... hanging by the
neck, twisted.
...
He removes her golden brooches, fingering them,
Holding them up,
Then rams the long pins into:
"Wicked, wicked eyes! You'll never know,
Never know my shame,
Go dark for all time,
Blind to what you should not have seen,
...
Now? This chant goes up: "Loved her, loved her,"
Each time striking once more, deep in, dripping, oozing
bloody muck –
It's caught in his beard –
"Loved her, loved her."
Such happiness.
Once. Now: "Catastrophe!
Throw wide the doors.
Let all Thebes see, father-killer, mother- ... no, too rank to say.
I AM THE PLAGUE!

I AM THE PLAGUE!
I AM THE PLAGUE!"
Look. The gates are opening." …
I thought I should ... familiarize myself with what she goes
through ... you know .... if I was going to actually play the
part. Anyway ... It's a beautiful translation.

(PAOLA and JEN exit the stage.)

   PAOLA. Chris Massaccio?
   CHRISTMAS. Right.
   JEN. Good luck.
   CHRISTMAS. Thanks.

(He and PAOLA go onstage. JEN falls apart.)

   PAOLA. Chris Masssssacio, Nathaniel Townsende.
   CHRISTMAS. Hey.
   NATHANIEL. Christmas?
   CHRISTMAS. No. Chris Massaccio.
   HAKIJA.   NATHANIEL.
Sorry.   Oh, oh.
   JEN. I'm sorry.
   NATHANIEL. Did you want to ask me anything?
   CHRISTMAS. Yeah, I did.
   HAKIJA. Didn't go well?
   CHRISTMAS.   JEN.
Uh—Oh, yeah, fate   It went really well. I'm sorry –
   NATHANIEL.
Yes.   JEN.
                       – forgive me.
   CHRISTMAS. But –

JEN. Oh god.

(She exits.)

CHRISTMAS. – I mean, I don't believe that, do you, that things are pre-determined?

NATHANIEL. Neither do they, they thought they were fated, big difference, but it doesn't matter what I believe, they believed it.

CHRISTMAS. But how do you make sense out of the play, then – like now?

NATHANIEL. *Like now?* Youuuu believe it while you're doing it.

CHRISTMAS. But still that leaves the audience going, "What the hell does this have to do with me?" / And what – ?

NATHANIEL. Well, b/ut –

PAOLA. We're running about –

NATHANIEL. By that logic, I'm, you're not wrong, it's a very good question, but you couldn't get anything from Hamlet, we don't believe in ghosts.

CHRISTMAS. Oh, I do. You don't believe in ghosts?

NATHANIEL.

Well, if – Look. Have you never found	
yourself doing things the same way you	
did them before even though they didn't	
work then and it makes no sense	
for you to do it that way,	
dating someone who	CHRISTMAS.
is really terrible—Well, there you go –	Ugh.
And in the same way the last really	... ...
terrible person for you –	Yes. ... ...
	don't even get
... ...	

Is that not a kind of fate?   [me –]
Some things defy reason:

    CHRISTMAS. Yes.

    NATHANIEL. War, drug addiction, my nosehair, these forces, smile please, deep, thank you, within us --

    CHRISTMAS. Yes.

    PAOLA. I think we have to ...

    NATHANIEL. To be continued. Okay, you're reading ...

    CHRISTMAS. Oh, um. Priest, Messenger –

    NATHANIEL. Good.

    CHRISTMAS. Herdsman, soothsayer guy, I'm sweating like a feckin' pig here.

    NATHANIEL. I see.

    CHRISTMAS. We're not supposed to take work outside the theater department, so, but –

    NATHANIEL. Well, if you're –

    CHRISTMAS. No, no, I'm sick of carrying spears, you know what I mean? Anyway, okay.

(He begins his audition. FANNY arrives in corridor.)

    FANNY. Are these the auditions? ... Is it just the two of us? ... What version did you bring? I'm sorry, are you preparing?

    HAKIJA. It's okay.

    FANNY. Oh god, did I bring the wrong one? Did it say that?

    HAKIJA. It's the best I could find.

    FANNY. How could you tell? Where are you from? You sound like you have an accent?

    HAKIJA. Where does it sound like I'm from?

    FANNY. I don't know, Russia? ... I have to guess.

HAKIJA. You could leave it a mystery.

FANNY. Oh, okay, uh ... Romania? Uhhhh, Yugoslavia? ... Yay! Isn't there, but, like a, sort of a *war* there?

HAKIJA. There is very much a war there.

FANNY. Oh. Is that why you're here? I'm sorry, I'm terribly nervous, this is the first time I've ever auditioned for a play set in *"olden"* times, I usually do newish, you know, contemporary things, so ... It helps to think about someone else, you want a shot? It's just wine, that's the only way I can get through these. I'm going to wind up like some old ... So tell me about your family, are they here too?

HAKIJA. What if I were to tell you they were all dead?

FANNY. Oh. My god, I'm sorry.

HAKIJA. I said, "What if I were to tell you?"

FANNY. Oh. Well ... Are they? I mean ... *What?*

HAKIJA. Myyyy ... mother and father are here.

FANNY. Oh good. Good for you. In Boston?

HAKIJA. ... My father and I lived for many years innnn ... *Vermont.*

FANNY. Oh, you've been here, I see. You're American. American Yugoslav.

HAKIJA. He is a carpenter. I was schooled at home.

FANNY. Oh. I, this, I really appreciate your talking to me, the less I think about this ... You're not like Bosnian.

HAKIJA. I am.

FANNY. Isn't that [where] – ? You speak beautiful English, the accent is very very faint.

HAKIJA. Most Europeans learn to speak English in their youth, even if I had grown up there.

FANNY. Yugoslavia is part of Europe? *(Pause.)* So ... just you and your father, what happened to your mother? Did you say?

HAKIJA. My mother, I was told abandoned me.

FANNY. Ohhhh.

HAKIJA. He's a taciturn fellow, my father, and rarely spoke except when teaching me. I was allowed to have friends over, but only when he was there, and I was not permitted to visit other people's homes or watch TV –

FANNY. Really?

HAKIJA. Well, we didn't have one, not even a radio. No newspapers.

FANNY. Wow. Did you, I don't know, go to church?

HAKIJA. Technically we are Muslims but my father is atheist, I am an atheist.

FANNY. I didn't know there were atheist Muslims.

PAOLA. *(To those in corridor.)* I'm sorry we're running so late, does anyone have to leave right away?

FANNY. Not me.

(PAOLA returns as CHRISTMAS reads the new speech.)

FANNY. Go on.

HAKIJA. I must have beennnnn, twelve, just, when he went to collect a piece of furniture, and I sneaked to a friend's house. My friend's mother asked if I wanted a glass of milk, and as she was pouring I saw a face of a boy on the milk carton, and a name, not mine, but a common Bosnian name, and my friend's mother asked what was wrong. Two days later a Sheriff arrived and arrested my father for kidnapping.

FANNY. No.

HAKIJA. He was not my father at all, but a man living in an area of Detroit inhabited by many other Muslims –

FANNY. No.

HAKIJA. – and he saw my mother abusing me; she was a

drunk and a pothead – I know, because I was returned to her, given my old name –

FANNY. Is this – ?

HAKIJA. She fell asleep smoking and burned half of our house down. Among other things. And my "father" was sent to prison where he is still serving a sentence.

FANNY.

Oh. My.

Go –

HAKIJA.

He'd wanted a child, saw me in danger, sold all of his possessions, snatched me, drove as far north as he could go near the border, bought a small tract of land, and

. . . .

. . . .

CHRISTMAS. *(A snippet:)*

"Catastrophe! Throw wide the doors – "

She, of course, would not let me go visit him; I couldn't tell her I loved him.

FANNY.

Did you love her? Too? ...

HAKIJA. She was a bad dream, an invention of fate. When I turned sixteen, I told her I was going to visit him in Attica whether she liked it or not; she just stood there like a stone statue with tears draining from it, and then whispered, "Let me send him a package, will you take it to him?" I told him I loved him and missed him and didn't blame him; he'd never abused me, he was my true father. I gave him the heavy paper sack, he opened it, never speaking a word, we parted, I ran away from home, came here.

CHRISTMAS. "... you may see for yourselves. Look: the gates are opening."

FANNY.

Good ...

NATHANIEL.
Good. Great. Very very nice.
We're running a little late –

... god.

CHRISTMAS.
Sure, sure, okay, thanks, good luck,
thanks. I mean –

Really.

PAOLA.

Hajika?

NATHANIEL.
Thanks.

HAKIJA.

Hakija.

CHRISTMAS. *(As he goes out.)*
You're welcome.

PAOLA. Hakija, sorry. Whenever you're ready. Sorry we're so behind.

(PAOLA returns to the stage.)

FANNY. Break a leg.
HAKIJA. Thank you.
FANNY. Can I ask ... what was in the paper bag?
HAKIJA. Oh. Horseshit, like the rest of the story.

(He goes into the theater.)

CHRISTMAS. Good luck with your audition. Mine sucked the big wet one.

Scene 3

(JEN and FANNY's apartment.)

FANNY.
"Horseshit. Just like the rest of the story." ... You think that's funny?

JEN.

Yeah. Isn't	FANNY.
it"	Never mind.
I'm sorry, it ..	... ...
W– ?	I thought it was real, I was upset for
... ...	him.
I'm sorry, you're right,	... ...
I see ...	Was I ... ? Maybe I don't have a
sense	
... ...	of humor, he was very very very
... ...	very creepoid.

It sounds it. *(Pause.)* But ...
I still think it's funny.

FANNY. I was vulnerable, I was about –

(Phone rings.)

FANNY. Hello? – No, wait, what number did you think you were – ? *(Hangs up)* They were in a fucking hurry, I was vulnerable, I was nervous, I was about to go in to audition,

it's like ...	JEN.
	You're,
... ...	you're right.
... it was my mother's	... ...
funeral and he came up to me	... ...
and kicked me in the groin or	... ...
something.	

... ...   Well ... yeah, not ... quite.

Look, no offense –

    JEN. How much have you had?

    FANNY. Don't do that, it's just wine. Some.

    JEN.

You've had some? Oh.   FANNY.

Some.   You, are not, a reliable, judge of

... ...   people, I think history bears this

... ...   out. You are drawn to these people.

Which ...   .

people?   Bad, bad people, bad men.

I married one bad man,

that doesn't ...

    FANNY. And what does that say about me, anyway, why did you pick me?

    JEN. Because you're bad?

    FANNY. Why didn't you just ... ? You're seven years older than me, why didn't you get your own place?

    JEN. I'm broke. You think I have terrible judgement.

    FANNY. They're not gonna call, they're not gonna call, I can't act. Why am I going to grad school? Why don't I just ... sign my life over to Wendy's? *(She turns on the TV: it's the news; she flips the channels.)* Look at all of these actors, they're all working, they're all getting paid, they're all beautiful or quirkily beautiful or related to someone famous and here I am waiting in knots in a tenement fucking apartment in the suburbs of Boston to find out if I can be allowed to please play an Elder for no money in an amateur production of a two million year old play. I mean, did you *read* it?

    JEN. Oedipus? I've, well, I've read it before.

    FANNY. "I've read it before."

JEN. Can we stop this?

FANNY. I mean, I don't know why we're supposed to like him, seriously. I don't want to be in it. If I think about it. Do I?

JEN. You don't have to like him, you have to feel terror and pity.

FANNY. Well, okay, then, why pity? Where's the pity? What's it for? He kills people who get in his way.

JEN. Yeah, but the gods shit all over him.

FANNY. So where's *our* play then?

JEN. I never know why people do mean things, though. I couldn't understand how Bart could be so mean about paying alimony after he was dumping *me*.

FANNY. Money and comfort, that's all everybody wants really.

JEN. Are you talking about him or me?

(Phone rings.)

FANNY. Hello? ... Just a sec.

JEN. Hi? ... Oh. Oh, great, wow. Thanks. Six thirty?, tomorrow?, sure, great, yeah, I know where it is. Thanks a lot. Bye.

FANNY. Your dentist?

JEN. I got the part.

FANNY. Great. Good. I'm really really really really happy.

JEN. Okay.

FANNY. I said I was happy.

JEN. Okay.

FANNY. You can only expect so much of people.

JEN. I said ok–

FANNY. I am not acting on my desire to hurt you. I don't
want to play an Elder.

(Phone rings.)

FANNY. Hello? This is she. Oh, great. Which, um, I
mean, how many Elders are there going to be in the chorus?
Thanks, bye. That's *First Elder* to you.

Scene 4

(Onstage. HAKIJA, JEN, FANNY, CHRISTMAS – who has
just arrived from class, breathless, not yet settled –
PAOLA, and NATHANIEL.)

FANNY.
"Oedipus the Tyrant, a new English adaptation from
Sophocles by Nathaniel Townsende III. In front of the palace
of Oedipus at ... "
        NATHANIEL. Thebes.
        FANNY. Right.
"Two generations before the Trojan War. To the right of the
stage near the altar stands the Priest with a crowd of
Thebans."
        NATHANIEL. Thebans.
        FANNY. Very good.
"Oedipus emerges from the central door."
        HAKIJA.
"Children, what are you doing here, pleading, bent down?"
Children?

NATHANIEL. Thebans. Or, also, implied: the audience, out there, children, hoping for easy entertainment, reaching up toward the light. *Kelp,* as it were. Imagine them waving in a deep pool, their lives lived in darkness. Whenever. Sorry.

HAKIJA.

"The city is burdened with moans, incense, intertwined,
I wouldn't trust a messenger, so came – ... Ah, so came to see with my own King's eyes." *"Turns to Priest?"* "You speak for them?"

CHRISTMAS.

"Our ship, the city of Thebes, can barely lift her prow – "

NATHANIEL. Prow.

CHRISTMAS.

" – *prow* from these bloody waves:
Plague dragging our, dragging down our people, drowning them in death.
You saved our city once.

You rid of
us the cursed–"

NATHANIEL.
"Once *before.*" "You rid us of–"

....   Take your time.

Where should I–?

NATHANIEL.

"You saved our city once before." And actually it's "Our city, the ship of Thebes."

CHRISTMAS.

"You saved our city once. Before.
You rid ... of us," it says.

NATHANIEL. That's a typo.

CHRISTMAS.

"You rid ooooo-us of the cursed Sphinx with the help of the gods, some say, And we beseech thee, help us once more.
If you don't, you will rule over a cit–an empty city."

NATHANIEL. Great.

HAKIJA.

"Yes, how I pity you, come filled with such wanting,

I know what is happening, for I bear the sorrow of you all,

I cannot sleep nor think of … but else.

I have sent Creon,

My brother in law, to the oracle.

He will learn how I may save this city.

He's been gone a long time.

When he returns, I swear I will do what Gods command,

or call me a villain and send me into exile."

    CHRISTMAS.   FANNY.

"He comes."   Foreshadow— *(Silent)* –ing, sorry.

    NATHANIEL.

See him first? Maybe?

    CHRISTMAS.

"He comes."

    HAKIJA.

"Creon?"

    CHRISTMAS.

"He looks pretty happy."

    HAKIJA.

"Brother, what news?"

    NATHANIEL.

"It is the guilt of murder that plagues our city.

We must drive out the polluted killer."

    HAKIJA.

"Well, who might he be? Are there clues as to his whereabouts?"

    NATHANIEL.

"The clues are here, right here before us, according to the Gods."

HAKIJA.
"Where did he die, the King?"
    NATHANIEL.
"He went by himself, never returned."
    HAKIJA.
"Was there no messenger, no traveling companion?"
    NATHANIEL.
"All killed, save one."
    HAKIJA.
"One?"
    NATHANIEL.
"He ran in fright, told us but one thing."
    HAKIJA.
"Which was?"
    NATHANIEL.
"That there were many robbers, many hands committeth the murder. How could these robbers have not backers from the city?"

FANNY.	NATHANIEL.
"Creon shrugs."	"The–" You don't have to read those. Thanks. You are *diligent!* "The Sphinx and her damnéd riddles kept us too busy to be solving crimes."

    HAKIJA.
"I will bring light to this darkness."

NATHANIEL.	FANNY.
"Exit all but the Chorus."	*"Exit all ... "*

Now, go very slowly with this,
the way I've broken it up–
    PAOLA. All right, all right.
    NATHANIEL. Fanny?

FANNY. What?

NATHANIEL. Do you understand how it's divided?

FANNY. We'll see.

PAOLA. "What does it mean?"

PAOLA & FANNY.

"What does it all mean? Gods, speak."

PAOLA.	FANNY.
"Athena –	"A–" That's me. But can I just ask?
	What do ... ? Are we two people?
	Do we represent ... more ... people?

NATHANIEL. Well. That's a really good question.

FANNY. Oh. Well, I feel better, thank you, but – what's the answer?

PAOLA.	NATHANIEL.
Maybe –	Let's – Let's explore it as we go, all
	right? Not jump to – The most
	powerful place artistically is not

FANNY.	*knowing....*
Oh.	....
....	Seriously. Out of that
....	everything else grows.

You sound like the Buddha.

"The power of not knowing."

NATHANIEL. I'm being serious. Look, I mean, I could tell you—

FANNY. No –

NATHANIEL. "The play's about this, the play's about that," do this, do that, but what good would that be?

FANNY. I was just–

NATHANIEL. You'd be doing it for me. But you're not here to please me, you're here to please yourself.

FANNY. Right.

NATHANIEL. Do you understand?

FANNY. No.

NATHANIEL. You don't?

FANNY. No, but I'm slow, it's not you.

NATHANIEL. Would you like it if I were to answer everything for you, tell you where to stand and sit and interpret the whole play?

FANNY. Sure.

NATHANIEL. Okay.

FANNY. Go on? "Athena, immortal daughter of Zeus:"

PAOLA.

"And Artemis, also daughter of Zeus, overseer of all wild things:"

FANNY & PAOLA.

"Forests, beasts, barbarous people, women."

PAOLA. I'm sorry, Nate.

NATHANIEL.

Can we – ?	PAOLA.
I just want to hear it. All ri – ?	But – I know, but I've
…	compared the other
	available translations–

This is an adaptation.

PAOLA. No, I know, but–"beasts, barbarous people, *women*–?"

NATHANIEL.

That was the attitude at	PAOLA.
the time. Let's just –	It isn't in Sophocles. Lloyd Jones
It's a free adaptation and	has–

the text is not up for discussion. Not now.

PAOLA. Then ... Oh, fine. You don't want to hear?

NATHANIEL. No, you think, what, that I didn't bother to look at the other translations,

PAOLA. No.

NATHANIEL.

I mean, all the other -- ?!?, before
I settled on this – you think I just,
what–?, pulled it all out of my ass?

PAOLA.
No.

PAOLA. No, I – Never mind.

NATHANIEL. No, go on, you've broken the rhythm – ,
we might as well –

PAOLA. You have Oedipus saying "You cannot think of
butt else." You have the Priest saying, "He looks pretty
happy!" It sound silly, honey.

NATHANIEL. I don't think it will sound "silly" in fact I
know it won't once it's played for its truth, there's deep
feeling under every moment. Let's take a break.

PAOLA. No, no, I said it, look, my name isn't going on it,
I'll say whatever you ask me to say.

NATHANIEL.

I really, this, I mean, if this is
your attitude on the first day, the
first hour –

....

....

PAOLA.
I only, if you don't
understand I'm trying
to save you humiliation –

We're taking a break.

PAOLA . I'm in your corner, Nate, I've said it –

NATHANIEL. Come outside with me.

PAOLA.

No. I'm through –

I'm through, if you want advice,
I'll give it, otherwise I'll shut up.

NATHANIEL.
Now? Please? Would you?

NATHANIEL. I'm not asking anyone to shut up.

PAOLA.

Well, I am. "Forests, beasts, barbarous people, women."

FANNY. Go on?

PAOLA & FANNY.

"And lastly, Apollo:

Purifier, ideal of young male beauty, watcher over music, archery, prophecy,

Medicine and the care of flocks and herds."

"Hear us, you three preventers of fate!"

NATHANIEL. Paola.

PAOLA. *(Perhaps laughing, losing some words.)* & FANNY.

"Our woes are infinite,

The ship of state is made of rotten wood.

No children are born, there is only death."

NATHANIEL. You're fucking fired.

PAOLA. Good luck everybody!

NATHANIEL. Paola—

PAOLA. Those goddam beasts and women, you know!

(She exits.)

NATHANIEL. Come back, I don't mean it, it's – Why doesn't everybody go for a ... ?

(He exits.)

CHRISTMAS. Wheeeeeeeeeee.

HAKIJA. You got the part.

JEN. The ... ?

HAKIJA. You got the part.

CHRISTMAS. I wonder if it's / going to be like this ...

JEN. What do you mean?

HAKIJA. You were upset about your audition.

JEN. *(To FANNY, mouthed.) What? (To Hakija.)* No. I was upset because it was good. I haven't acted in seven years.

HAKIJA. No?

JEN. I gave it up for somebody I adored, and who seemed to need me much more than I needed it, and after I put him through the rest of medical school, I took a job as a pharmacist's assistant which I am *still* doing, believe it or not, he dumps me for his, yes, ladies and germs, his secretary whom he had impregnated, and at that point I was actually pregnant after trying for seven *years.* So I had an abortion and here we find ourselves at ... What shall we call this? Skit Night In Dixie.

HAKIJA. Not so funny.

JEN. Well, no.

HAKIJA. You make a joke.

(PAOLA and NATHANIEL return.)

NATHANIEL. Okay, we're back. Look, everyone, it isn't that I don't want your feedback, I do, your suggestions, but not – come to me individually, all right? *(To PAOLA.)* You okay?

PAOLA. Just go on.

NATHANIEL. That way we won't be taking up the other actors' time hammering out changes. But I want your thoughts, your questions, this is a collective process, and I believe foremost in process. We're going to discover, *together,* what this thing is. So, let's start with Oedipus's next speech.

FANNY. We didn't finish our –

NATHANIEL. Oh, yes, right, the Chorus, from ...

FANNY.

"In the countless deaths–" *(To Paola.)* You ready?

"In the countless – "

FANNY & PAOLA.

" – deaths."

FANNY.

"The children born without – "

PAOLA & FANNY.

" – breath."

FANNY.

"Cold from the – "

FANNY & PAOLA.

" – womb."

FANNY.

"White-haired women and wives bend to you with prayer:"

FANNY & PAOLA.

"Save us!

Our enemy is Zeus,

Drive him out, drive him back!

Banish Zeus from our hometown!"

NATHANIEL. *What?*

PAOLA. Honey, Zeus isn't the, no, I'm sorry, we'll talk about it later –

NATHANIEL. Zeus, isn't the *what?,* please? I'm asking you.

PAOLA. I thought ... You've misread, Zeus isn't the enemy, King Laius's killer is the enemy, Zeus is being called on to get rid of the jerk. I mean ...

NATHANIEL. All right, we'll look at it. I am perfectly capable of admitting that I can make a mistake. Clearly.

PAOLA. What does that mean?

NATHANIEL.
"Oedipus returns."

HAKIJA.	FANNY.
"The thing – "	*"Oedipus – "*
... ...	Sorry.
"The—"	*"Oedipus returns."*

"[The] thing you ask of me,

if you will hear and embrace my words,

fight the plague with me,

you will discover the courage to banish all this suffering ...

I am a stranger to this story and to this act of murder.

If any man knows whose hand it was that slayeth Laius –

Slayeth Laius ... "

    NATHANIEL.

Slayed Laius. No, that ... felled ... "If any man knows whose hand it was that ... "

    HAKIJA.

"–slaughtered the King ... "

    NATHANIEL.

"–slaughtered the... slaughtered *Laius,* no slaughtered the King... "

    HAKIJA.

" – slaughtered Laius – "

    NATHANIEL. Okay?

    HAKIJA.

"I, I am a stranger to this story and to this murderous act. If any man – "

    NATHANIEL. "This act of – " No, that's better, you're right, sorry, go on.

    HAKIJA.

"If any man knows whose hand it was that slaughtered Laius, I command him speak."

NATHANIEL. Him, good, Hajika.
HAKIJA.

Hakija.

"And if he is afraid to incriminate   NATHANIEL.
himself, I promise no bitter punishment: God, fuck, I even
He may *depart* our city unharmed."   practiced it.

    NATHANIEL. Depart, better.
    PAOLA. Christ.
    NATHANIEL. Sh.

(PAOLA exits during:)

    HAKIJA.
"If he knows the killer to
   be a foreigner,
I command him speak.   NATHANIEL.
But if he keeps silence,   Paola ... Paola ...
To protect himself or a friend,   Oh great ...
For any reason,   … … …
Here is what I shall do:"   … … …

… … …   Go on. You're doing
… … …   wonderfully.
… … …   Really.
"Here– Here is what I shall do: Wonderfully. Sorry.
Here me!

Let no man shelter him, no man feed him, nor speak to him,
nor give him water to wash his face,
Let no one include him in any sacrifice, any prayer,
May he be banished, driven out, *unseen,*
his life in exile, cursed everywhere he goes."

    NATHANIEL. He's cursing himself!

HAKIJA.

"Whoever did this deed, know that you are never to be at home anywhere,

Always to wander, filthy and abhorred.

And if I should learn he lives in the confines of *my own home,*

May I *then* be so cursed, banished, doomed! Yes!

Since I now wear his crown

And have his Queen for my wife—"

(PAOLA re-enters.)

PAOLA.What is so patently disgusting to me –
NATHANIEL. Out.
PAOLA.

Is that I have to save up my
suggestions for bettering the text
but this one gets to suggest
anything he likes, it is so
transparent how much you
want to blow him, why don't
you just get down on your knees
now and we can all get it over
with. You moron, you hypocrite,
you asked me to help you.

NATHANIEL.
Paola. *Paola* ...
Okay. Great.
... Go ...
You're humiliating
no one but ...
... ...

... ...

His dick is this big.

(As she is exiting once more:)

NATHANIEL. Well, more like ...

(Jokingly he approximates something only slightly larger as he starts to follow PAOLA out.)

Scene 5

(Bus. FANNY and JEN.)

FANNY. That was him.

JEN. Who?

FANNY. Oedipus. The guy who told me that story. At the audition.

JEN. Oh.

FANNY. Worrisome, no?

JEN. No. Yeah.

(Add: A bar. CHRISTMAS and HAKIJA.)

CHRISTMAS. This okay?

JEN. What was it again?

FANNY.

Horseshit, just like the	JEN.
rest of the story.	Right right.

Weren't you listening when I ... ?

JEN. No, I was, it's, I mean–

CHRISTMAS. That's okay.

JEN. – you have to admit, –

HAKIJA. You sure?

JEN. – that was some major horseshit

tonight, that's all.	CHRISTMAS.
I'm thinking.	You get the next one.

HAKIJA. Okay.

FANNY. You were never away from him long enough to tell you.

JEN. I wasn't? Well, there wasn't anywhere to go. That theater is where we go when we die if we've been bad.

FANNY. Too late to back out?

JEN. No.

CHRISTMAS. Man.

JEN. Not at all. I would if ... No, not at all.

FANNY. If you were me?

JEN. No no.

FANNY. Why me?

CHRISTMAS. That was ...

JEN. I don't know, I didn't say that. Because, well, you have two lines.

HAKIJA. Yeah.

JEN. At least I'm playing, I mean, look, the whole thing is nuts.

FANNY. You think I should quit.

JEN. No.

HAKIJA. Funny.

JEN. I was, *I* would probably –

CHRISTMAS. Shit.

JEN. Yes. I don't know, I'm not you, though.

CHRISTMAS. Do you think the translation is so bad?

HAKIJA. No.

CHRISTMAS. Me either.

FANNY. There is something very ...

CHRISTMAS. And ...

FANNY. ... *very* wrong with that guy.

JEN. Nate?

CHRISTMAS.

CHRISTMAS.	JEN.
... are they a couple?	Oh. Yeah. Good actor, though. *(Pause.)* But
... ...	... ...
I think he's sort of sexy.	
... ...	... yeah, he is .... very ...

I'd do him.

... ...

I'm not exactly clear on how
he sees the play, but ...

... ...

Are you?

... ...

intense, kind of.

... ...

... ...

That's sort of the part ...

... ...

... though.

HAKIJA. I'm not sure he is either.

CHRISTMAS. So ... You're ... where are you from? Originally?

HAKIJA. Bosnia.

CHRISTMAS. Yeowch.

JEN. ... Are you mad at me?

FANNY. Why?

CHRISTMAS. Sorry.

JEN. 'Cause I said I would quit?

FANNY. No.

CHRISTMAS. I mean ...

FANNY. Just don't sleep with him.

JEN. Please.

CHRISTMAS. Wow.

JEN. Or because I didn't ... remember ...

FANNY. No. Please.

CHRISTMAS. Glad you're here.

FANNY. I'm not that ...

CHRISTMAS. And not there.

(Add: NATHANIEL's apartment. NATHANIEL and PAOLA.)

NATHANIEL.
Paola?

... ...

JEN.
You're sure?

Paola?

    CHRISTMAS. How long? You ... been here?

    HAKIJA. Six months.

    NATHANIEL. Let me in.

    CHRISTMAS. Are ... ? Can I ask?

    NATHANIEL. Honey?

    CHRISTMAS. Are ... ? You're straight, right?

    HAKIJA. Americans think it makes people less myster-
ious if you give them a name.

    CHRISTMAS. You're right.

    JEN. Thanks.

    CHRISTMAS. We do.

    HAKIJA. Your movies and books all purport to explain
human beings.

    NATHANIEL. I'm pouring a drink, do you want one?

    HAKIJA. You can't explain human beings.

    CHRISTMAS. Here's to that.

    PAOLA. I hate you.

    CHRISTMAS. To mystery!

    NATHANIEL. I'm aware.

    HAKIJA. Tchin tchin.

    NATHANIEL. Here's your drink. You've already had
some, haven't you?

    PAOLA. Fuck you.

    NATHANIEL. All right. If that'll fix it.

    PAOLA. No – You cast that ... *milkmaid* as Jocasta, she
was *fine* as the Messenger, but ... You wouldn't even let me
see the script, I'm so ...

    NATHANIEL. I know.

    PAOLA. ... *humiliated.*

    NATHANIEL. I'm sorry.

    PAOLA. Why did you do that?

NATHANIEL. I just wanted to hear it once without a lot of criticism.

(Pause.)

CHRISTMAS. But are you?

PAOLA. I'll be good.

CHRISTMAS. I mean –

PAOLA. I felt so exposed.

CHRISTMAS. You don't have to ...

PAOLA. I'm the only Equity actor there –

CHRISTMAS. I mean, I'm not trying to explain you.

PAOLA. – I'm supposed to be your co-director, you didn't mention that to anyone –

FANNY. I think it could be good.

JEN. You do?

PAOLA. – you so obviously found that child –

FANNY. I do.

PAOLA. – I don't know –

NATHANIEL. I didn't, though –

JEN. Yeah.

NATHANIEL. – you imagined that.

JEN. Maybe.

PAOLA. Whatever.

CHRISTMAS. To mystery!

PAOLA. Cheers.

JEN. It could, I think.

PAOLA. You just tell me what you want, you know I'll do it.

NATHANIEL. No, we're partners.

PAOLA. No, we're not.

NATHANIEL. Yes.

PAOLA. No.

JEN. Let's stick in there for a while.

NATHANIEL. Yes.

FANNY. Why not?

JEN. What the hell.

PAOLA. No. "Banis h Zeus from our *hometown?"*

NATHANIEL. That was awkward. Our city?

CHRISTMAS. Did you think I was? Straight or ... ? Bi?

PAOLA. ... It'll be a very beautiful production –

CHRISTMAS. No.

PAOLA. People are terrified –

CHRISTMAS. No –

PAOLA. – of Greek tragedy –

CHRISTMAS. I don't want to know.

PAOLA. – you'll throw them against the wall and nail them.

CHRISTMAS. Seriously. Here's to mystery. I mean it!

PAOLA. Right here. In your own hometown.

NATHANIEL. Shut up.

PAOLA. ... I'm glad you're finally doing something.

(Pause.)

NATHANIEL. Yeah. Can we be? Please? Partners?

PAOLA. Oh, of course. I'm sorry.

NATHANIEL. They'll see I don't know anything.

PAOLA. Of course you know something.

HAKIJA. So ...

PAOLA. I love you.

HAKIJA. You're dyslexic.

NATHANIEL. I love you, too.

CHRISTMAS. You could tell?

NATHANIEL. God.

Scene 6

(Rehearsal. All assembled.)

NATHANIEL. Listen up. New pages. As I've said, we'll continue to get stuff as my co-adaptor and co-director and I –

PAOLA. Okay.

NATHANIEL. – work our way through the text. Your patience is hugely appreciated, again: process, process, process; you are an immensely talented crew, and we are both of us more excited than we may appear at having you all collaborate with us, dig, seek out the deeper truth in this ...

PAOLA. Et cetera.

NATHANIEL.

Okay. Page ...	JEN.
whatever, help me ...	Pretty blouse. Really really-
someone ...	
fucking ... Why don't I have an –	
CHRISTMAS.	PAOLA.
You motherfucker. Joke.	Sixteen. You do have an.
Mother–	
NATHANIEL.	HAKIJA.
Okay – This is one of those	Got it.
places where the condensation	
is most severe.	

JEN. Right.

NATHANIEL. I want this production to feel like a bullet going right into the wound –

JEN. Oh, yeah?

NATHANIEL. Not only making it but flying out the other side and splattering the wall with the audience's guts and brains.

FANNY. Yum.

NATHANIEL. Where we left off.

FANNY.

"Teiresias, the blind prophet of Apollo."

HAKIJA.

"Yes, I have sent for him."

FANNY.

"Here he comes: the only man – "

PAOLA & FANNY.

"Here he comes: the only man for whom truth is second nature."

NATHANIEL. I don't think he wears a blindfold.

CHRISTMAS. I'm trying to figure out what it's like to be –

NATHANIEL. Good. Great, good idea.

HAKIJA.

"Teiresias, you see more than any other man, though you are blind.

Spare us none of your knowledge,

Save us, save your city,

Save me."

NATHANIEL. Good.

CHRISTMAS.

"Knowledge is worthless if save you it can't."

NATHANIEL.

" – if it cannot save you."

CHRISTMAS.

"If it cannot save you." Sorry. "I knew this – "

NATHANIEL. I know.

CHRISTMAS. No, that's the line. "I knew this, but tried to know it not – "

NATHANIEL. Unknow it, no "not."

CHRISTMAS.

"*Un*know it, no ... " ... "I knew this – "

NATHANIEL. Take a break everyone, we'll work on this for a bit –

CHRISTMAS. "I knew this, / but tried to –"

NATHANIEL. – then resume, ask Paola questions, this is all good, great work. I mean it, really, you're all incredible. Okay. It's fine.

CHRISTMAS. I know.

NATHANIEL. Breathe.

CHRISTMAS. I'll get it.

NATHANIEL. Christmas.

CHRISTMAS. I will, I promise.

NATHANIEL. *Merry* Christmas.

CHRISTMAS. Ho ho.

NATHANIEL. Have some fun.

CHRISTMAS. Oh.

NATHANIEL. You didn't have any problem at the audition.

CHRISTMAS. I'd memorized it, that's all, I'll memorize this.

NATHANIEL. Okay.

JEN. So ...

CHRISTMAS. This always happens.

NATHANIEL. Is there anything I'm doing that–?

JEN. Oh.

CHRISTMAS. No no no no no.

NATHANIEL. Or anything you'd like me to?

JEN. Thanks.

CHRISTMAS. No. I mean ... I'd love to ... have a drink with you some night but –

JEN. Great.

NATHANIEL. Sure. Sure sure sure. Of course. Let's ... ...

JEN. You, uh ...

NATHANIEL. Let's just read it slowly, all right?

FANNY. So you worked / on the translation?

JEN. No thanks. / Thanks.

HAKIJA. Hm?

FANNY. How long have you known Nate?

JEN . You know ...

PAOLA. We met during the Pleistocene.

JEN. ... you kind of –

FANNY. Is that a Greek play?

JEN. – you kind of freaked my friend out at the audition...

HAKIJA. Why did you make a joke about what happened to you?

JEN. When? Oh, th[e other—] ? I don't know. Because it's sad.

HAKIJA. It's not sad.

JEN. No?

HAKIJA. It's tragic.

JEN. Oh, well – I knew who he was, even though, I mean, yes, I thought he hung the moon, but I was also probably making some kind of bargain with myself: I could have a beautiful life, he'd make a lot of money and our children would be safe, but I wasn't, I mean, I don't think I was a victim. What? ... And killing your father and fucking your mother is tragic, my story is ... What's that?

HAKIJA. Americans. You all think ... mortal creatures

can win.

JEN. Well –

HAKIJA. An amazing ability.

JEN. Not ... *all* Americans ...

HAKIJA. In my experience. You are – more than you think, yes ... much more ... like our Oedipus:

JEN. How?

HAKIJA. Blind to your own tragedy, not to mention ...

JEN. Well ... Maybe so. Mention ... ? ...

HAKIJA. Anyone else's.

JEN. Right. *(Pause.)* Well ... so ... were you trying to be funny at the audition when you told that story to Fanny?

HAKIJA. Anything anyone says to someone named Fanny should be funny, don't you think?

JEN. Were you?

HAKIJA. Your friend asked me if there wasn't "like a sort of a war going on" in my country.

JEN. Uh-huh? ... Well ...You must be used to that ... by now? ... I don't know, I'm only making conversation, that's –

HAKIJA. No. Not to put too fine a point on it – or risk bringing anyone down – but two hundred thousand of my countrymen, including all of my family, were slaughtered in full view of the world. Our Christian neighbors, who have known us since childhood, for generations – and mind you, these are not peasants, poor people, these are doctors and successful businessmen and lawyers and scientists, my father was a Professor of Philosophy, *indistinguishable* from you or me if you were to see them – which you couldn't or refused to, I won't speak for you, Americans refused – these people, friends, colleagues, simply because they had Serbian ancestry and we were Muslims, came into our homes, murdered many of the men, raped the women and drove the survivors into camps where most starved to death. That is not, nowhere near the worst. If I were to tell you the worst of what I saw, you would say I was inventing it. Not possible.

JEN. I'm sorry.

HAKIJA. The only people in the world capable of putting a stop to any of this left an embargo on all weapons to one side, ours, and stood by, using so-called Humanitarian Efforts to excuse themselves from doing anything.

JEN. I'm as ignorant as –

HAKIJA. Of course. You're, as I said, interested in winning. If we agree, *together*, not to see something, then ... Well. And just to be perfectly clear: an American is what I want very much to become; it is only because of American Relief efforts, private –

JEN. Yes.

HAKIJA. I am alive at all. So. You mustn't give it another thought. I'll apologize to your ... Fanny.

JEN. No ... I ...

HAKIJA. That was a joke.

JEN. Oh. Yes.

PAOLA. Okay, we're back.

HAKIJA.
To the blind! May we all be so lucky.
...

NATHANIEL.
Where we left off? Top of whatever the fuck...ing*fuck*...

PAOLA.
Here.

HAKIJA.
'For godsakes tell us what you know, we're on our knees to you!"

CHRISTMAS.
"They are your troubles, not mine."
NATHANIEL. Shh!

FANNY.
Getting acquainted?

HAKIJA.
"You would betray us, keep this knowledge hidden?"
     CHRISTMAS.
     "Time the all-seeing will find you out again[st your will!]"
     HAKIJA.
"What is your secret?"
     CHRISTMAS.
Sorry, sorry, uhhhh,
"You are the murderer of the king,
You are the enemy you seek.
You live in filthy shame with your loved ones."
     HAKIJA.

"Do you begin	CHRISTMAS.
to imagine that you	"You are a pathetic wretch to use
will ever	these words that soon upon, that
escape me?	soon will rain on you!"

Your life is darkness,
You cannot hurt me or any man
who sees the light."
     CHRISTMAS.
"It is you – "
     HAKIJA.
"NO MORE! Did Creon put you up to this?
How much? How much did he pay you, stinking *old man*?!?
When the Sphinx held your countrymen in chains, did you
speak?
Did you have the answers then?
How convenient you can see the gods' truths now.
Putrefying in your last sick days,
Take your money, take your shame,
Go back to Creon and bow down to him,
On the floor, on your knees,

Serve him however you can,
The two of you in foulest damnest blindness,
I answered her, I stopped the Sphinx, not you,
WHERE WERE YOU THEN?
With my wit, my brains alone,
With *thinking,* not magic! I did it!
I rid this land of that riddling bitch!
With no powers but my own,
Did you witness that?
You claim Apollo on your side,
Run to him now, beg Apollo to save you,
I'll show you what you gain by this treason,
I'll show you things you can't imagine
I'll do it, Oedipus the King!"
    CHRISTMAS.
"The Tyrant! Not King, Tyrant!"
    PAOLA & FANNY.
"Stop, you both speak in anger."
    CHRISTMAS.
"Pour your hatred on me–" Did I hit you? "–the fates shall grind you down to nothing, Fool!"
    NATHANIEL. Okay, okay, that's ... *Good Christ.*
    FANNY. Scary.
    PAOLA. Loud. Kidding. It was great.
    JEN. It really – ...
    NATHANIEL. Okay –
    CHRISTMAS. Gee, thanks. He he.

Scene 7

(Lunch. All but NATHANIEL.)

CHRISTMAS. So does Nate have, do you think, like a concept that Oedipus relates to something more ... current, do you think?

PAOLA. More – ? I think – well, first of all, you should ask him. But I suspect he'll say he wants the play to speak for itself.

CHRISTMAS.

But I mean like, yeah, but, like ...	FANNY.
sometimes I can't tell if he's ...	I –
but –	I –
Go ahead.	... ...
... .	No. You.

Is there a point?, a particular point
of view on the play? We should all ... ?

PAOLA. Well, I think he's kind of traditional, but I don't want to speak for him.

JEN. But if Oedipus is America? Say. *(To HAKIJA.)* Do you want to ... ? And the chorus is the ongoing debate among the populace about what's the best course of action like we used to have before TV made everything one big opinion, annnnd Jocasta is the conservative because she doesn't want Oedipus to ask any more questions ... This isn't my idea really.

FANNY. Whose is it?
JEN. Do ... ?
FANNY. Idea?
JEN. Paola?
FANNY. Hello?

PAOLA. Oh, I hadn't thought about any of that, frankly, I'm still ...

FANNY. I'd just like to know if –

JEN. We heard.

FANNY. I'm asking about something else now.

JEN. Oh. Sorry.

FANNY. If you and I are one voice or our own voices.

PAOLA. I agree. Let's try it both ways.

JEN. But the idea of responsibility, refusing to accept any–

CHRISTMAS. Yes.

JEN. –blaming everyone else, striking out, ridiculing, isolating them, insinuating, metaphorically or even literally killing them and never stopping to ask: What about me? What have I done? What am I doing to make things worse?

CHRISTMAS. If Oedipus is America and the Chorus is the voting populace, say, and Jocasta is the, whatever, right of center sort of –

HAKIJA. Reactionary.

CHRISTMAS. Then Teiresias ... ?

HAKIJA. Sees the truth. The petty egos involved.

JEN. Yes.

HAKIJA. He sees through all the lies and knows who is to blame. And says so. These people are always dismissed or jailed, in wartime or any crisis it is not allowed for anyone to say no, to disagree.

JEN & CHRISTMAS. Right.

HAKIJA. They become traitors.

JEN & CHRISTMAS. Right.

FANNY. You two should do Greek chorus work.

HAKIJA. Laws are written to silence them; they become more hated than the enemy; and when the war is over everyone agrees to forget what was done to them and who did it.

JEN. *(To us.)* You could practically warm your hands by him.

Scene 8

(Rehearsal, in medias res.)

FANNY.
"Jocasta –   JEN.
– enters." Oh, okay, sorry.   "STOP!"
     CHRISTMAS.
"You'll learn so many things: your true parents, your true acts.
"You shall see who you are, with you [*he has meant to say
"With who? and believes he has actually said it.]* you in, live
with, and in what horror!"
     FANNY & PAOLA.
"Who is the man who–?"
     CHRISTMAS. Nate?
     NATHANIEL. Yes.
     CHRISTMAS. Sorry. We were talking at lunch? About
what this, how this, you know, might be something we could
connect to in relation to now? Or how to ... Anyway, do you
think that Teiresias is like ... say a kind of left wing, or
dissident –

     NATHANIEL. No, no, no, no, please don't go there,
please don't, let's not do that, okay, can we just agree we're
going to not try to make the fucking play *relevant* as if it isn't
already. Let people, I mean, give *them* the courtesy and
respect of letting them make those connections.

     CHRISTMAS. Oh, okay, yeah, I –

FANNY. The kelp, you mean?

NATHANIEL. Fate requires Oedipus to kill his father and his mother, and he tries to escape that fate, Teiresias reminds him that he cannot, he still goes into total denial mode, and he destroys himself. Left wing dissident. I love you, come here. You are very precious. If anything, Teiresias is the Wall Street Journal telling everybody what is completely obvious if they would get their heads out of their buttholes: America is fated to be an Empire. That's our true fate.

PAOLA. Pretend you're on the Riviera. I do.

NATHANIEL. We got all the natural resources, we have the money and the military might and anybody who pretends that doesn't come with tremendous responsibilities and problems is a moron. The use of power is inherent in our existence. If we were really smart, we would just blow up anybody who doesn't get that.

PAOLA. Look at all the pretty bathing suits!

NATHANIEL. Even if it is our fate, we still have to choose it, it isn't pre-determined, you see?

CHRISTMAS. No.

NATHANIEL. You are by far the cutest Teiresias in theatre history, I would concentrate on that.

CHRISTMAS. Okay. I will.

NATHANIEL. Father Christmas, let's start with line ... oh, what's the goddam, "suffering" what is it? "Cause of ... ?"

HAKIJA.

"He says I am the cause of all our suffering!"

NATHANIEL.

Thank you.

JEN.

"He knows this first hand or he was told?"

HAKIJA.

"He claims he speaks for Apollo."

JEN.

"Forget these ideas, and hear me out, learn, Oedipus, for I can
teach you something from my experience:

No prophecies are real. I'll prove it.

Once, long ago, an oracle claiming to speak for the gods told
Laius that someday he would die at the hands of his very own
son, our son, and that our child would marry me, bearing sons
from a son.

But our son did not live."

HAKIJA.

"You had a son?"

JEN.

"One. At three days old his ankles pierced, *pinned,* crippling
him,

And left upon a barren hill far away from here.

The prophecy is unfulfilled, can't you see?"

NATHANIEL.

"Can't *you* see?"

JEN.

Oh. "Can't you see?"

NATHANIEL. No, no – It's for him, it's to him –

JEN. Oh, oh.

NATHANIEL. – now don't make it all about yourself –

JEN. Right right.

NATHANIEL. – forget your feelings—

JEN. Yes.

NATHANIEL. – achieve your actions, / play them.

JEN.

Good. I – yes.

"Laius was killed by strangers, not a son, at some place where

three roads meet.
Leave these fears behind--
What's wrong?
The gods do what they will, not what these oracles predict."
    HAKIJA.
"Three roads, you say, that meet? In what country, where?"
    JEN.
"W--In Phocia."
    HAKIJA.
"How long ago?"
    JEN.
"What's wrong?"
    HAKIJA.
"How long, woman?"
    JEN.
"Just, uh, well, just before you ... "
    HAKIJA.
"BEFORE?!?!?!"
    JEN.
"You came to us. Don't HAKIJA.
frighten me.   "Oh Zeus, what will you have of me?
What? What is it?"
    HAKIJA.
"Nothing. Tell me of Laius --   JEN.
How tall, how old, hurry up!" "What of ... ? Tall, his hair
...   going gray, like yours, his
...   build, not at all unlike yours."
"I've cursed myself!"
    JEN.
"What?"
    NATHANIEL.
Ask him.

HAKIJA.   JEN.
"I've, what, are you deaf?   *"What?"*
HAKIJA.
"Who brought the news, how did you learn of his death?!"
JEN.
"One servant who escaped alone, but stop, please, you're frightening – "
HAKIJA.
"Where is he now?"
JEN.
He saw you on the throne, he ran, what does all this mean?"
HAKIJA.
"Nothing, I told you."
JEN.
"Nothing? He, he touched my sleeve and begged me send him out into some far off pasture, far from here."
HAKIJA.
"We must see him, have him back."
JEN.
"But why?"
HAKIJA.
"I fear I have said too much."
JEN.
"To your own wife?"
HAKIJA.
"Fetch him, fetch him now!"
JEN.
"This does not seem like nothing!"
HAKIJA.
"I won't believe it so   JEN.
until I see?:   Believe what?"
the wickedness within, I won't see it,

won't call it by a name till it stands there naked and
exposed ... otherwise, it does not exist. *Go!"*

JEN.

"If this be nothing, may I never know a thing." Better?
NATHANIEL. ... We'll get there.

Scene 9

(A bar. All six.)

PAOLA. Why would someone – No, no, hear me out –
someone who'd been warned specifically that he was going to
kill his father and marry his mother ever kill anyone or marry
anyone, at all?!, do you see what I'm saying? You're just
asking for trouble.

CHRISTMAS. But he – He thinks he knows his parents,
but he doesn't.

PAOLA. Yessssss, but still, if you wanted, you see, he's
rash – he's a rash person –

NATHANIEL. That's not his flaw, rashness, plus it's not
a flaw in the sense of character failing. The whole idea of
tragic "flaw" is crap.

CHRISTMAS. Really?

NATHANIEL. Plus –, Yes! and it's not about guilt, no
one is being punished—

CHRISTMAS. But-

PAOLA. Well he's right, the tragic "flaw" is no more
than an error in judg—

JEN.	PAOLA.
	(sound dropping out on:)
What is wrong?	– ment, a foolish act, Oedipus
	pronouncing the curse on himself,

FANNY.
Nothing.

JEN.
Stop it.
It's not what
you think.
You should
talk to him.

FANNY.
No thank you.

JEN.
Why?

FANNY.
Because I think
he's scary.
Not. A nice. Person.
JEN.
He's been through an awful
lot.
FANNY.
He says.

JEN.
What does that ... ?

and/or thinking he knows who his
real parents are.
CHRISTMAS.
And his pride.

NATHANIEL.   PAOLA.
No!   Well, no.

CHRISTMAS.
No?

PAOLA.
Pride was not a sin in ancient
Greece.

CHRISTMAS.
No?

NATHANIEL & PAOLA.
No.   No.

NATHANIEL.
Not at all. Pride was a virtue.
Hubris was a sin.
PAOLA.
Or hybris.
CHRISTMAS.
What's the difference?
NATHANIEL.
Madame?

FANNY.
I can say I'm a ballerina, it doesn't mean I am. Go. Enjoy him. Maybe he'll tell you an interesting story.

PAOLA.
Hybris is, means literally water overflowing its bounds, but it means figuratively to treat the less powerful, the weak, unfairly, to bully them, beat them down the way Oedipus speaks to Tereisias and the

JEN.
I wish –

Messenger and the Herdsman, but –

FANNY. I'm not your mother, it's fine.

CHRISTMAS. That's hubris?

FANNY. Trust your instincts. Deeply *flawed* — as they are.

CHRISTMAS. Did you all know that hubris is not pride? It's bullying the weak and powerless! Why don't they teach you that?

JEN. Why don't they teach you that Columbus didn't discover America and was a genocidal maniac?

NATHANIEL. Oh, yes, and you'd be where doing what now if we'd said, "Oh, sorry, Mr. Indian, it's your country, bye, we'll go back to England and be burned at the stake for having different religious beliefs?

PAOLA. Oh, please, don't even listen to him ...

NATHANIEL. Enjoy!"

JEN.
So wait. You think our good fortune now justifies that slaughter of an entire civilization?

PAOLA.
Okay: a drunk tells him that Polybus and Merope are not his real parents and Oedipus runs to the oracle to find out the truth –

CHRISTMAS. Right.

NATHANIEL. Yep.

PAOLA. And the oracle tells him he's going to kill his dad and marry his mom, *but* –

JEN. A whole continent.

NATHANIEL. I'm happy. I didn't have to do it. Fuck 'em.

JEN. Oh, yeah, well. Good, great.

                                        PAOLA.
                                        I promise
                                        you
                                        he's only
                                        trying to
                                        see
                                        how deep
                                        your capacity
                                        for disgust
                                        goes.
                                        San Tropez!
                                        (To CHRISTMAS.)
HAKIJA.   But since
You okay?   this isn't
                                        what he
                                        wanted
                                        to hear,
                                        he totally ignores
JEN.   the earlier
                                        information
Oh yeah. 'Americans!'... How   that his real
are you doing?   parents might be

HAKIJA.
Okay. I guess. Learning a lot.

JEN.
Oh good. *(Silence between them. She notices a book in his jacket or bag.)*
Marx?

HAKIJA.
Required reading.

JEN.
For an actor?

HAKIJA.
I am economics major.

elsewhere and races away from his adoptive parents, killing the very first man he meets at a crossroads and marrying the very first woman he meets in Thebes.

FANNY.
So Nate?

PAOLA.
I mean, he isn't acting in any
sense reasonably, is he? He's
acting crazy and telling himself he's being rational, don't you see?

JEN. Really?

NATHANIEL. *(Over JEN and HAK.)* Who are you arguing with?

JEN. Seriously? Wow.

PAOLA. *(Over)* I'm not arguing – Don't –I'm only –

NATHANIEL. *(Over JEN and HAK.)* I know, just, just checking.

PAOLA. It's the most modern thing about –

JEN. But you've studied acting.

PAOLA. *(Continuous, over.)* –the play: what human beings don't want to know, they just ...

JEN. Yes you have.

PAOLA. – literally, allow themselves to not know.

HAKIJA. I am very bad liar, trust me.

CHRISTMAS. This is so cool.

NATHANIEL. Hak? ...

CHRISTMAS. I never would have thought of that.

NATHANIEL. Hak. *(Sees TV overhead.)* Tahoe. We've been there.

PAOLA.
He's abandoned on a
hillside with his feet *pinned*
together, he's even named for
it, Oiedin pous, "Swell
Foot",
it was common knowledge
then that that people who
didn't want their
children pinned
their feet together and left
them to die ...
But!

NATHANIEL.
You know I think you're the
farthest thing from that.

JEN.
He's an economics major,
he's never studied acting.

NATHANIEL.
Nuh-uhn. You're
shitting me.

... ...   JEN.

No.
Apparently.
Oh, forget eco-   not.
fuckin-omics,
you're gonna be a star.

PAOLA. *(Cont.)*
He doesn't even ask *himself*
why he's named that. Like ...   JEN.
okay: it would be like if my   I agree.

name were "Paola Dumped
in the Sea," you think I'd be
sort of curious.
Wouldn't you?

CHRISTMAS.
Pretty name though.
Yeah, abso/lu—

PAOLA.
But: no curiosity!
All he has to do is stop and
add up the clues! He's a
Know-It-All. Today he'd be
a *pundit*.

CHRISTMAS.
Right, right, right,
But – but he still couldn't
stop it from –
because of *Fate*. Right?

PAOLA.
He i--, yes, but he is
actively keeping
himself from
knowing what he

NATHANIEL.
Economics? Look, seriously
I'll, Hak, I will be more
than happy to
give you names,
references to
to the best agents
and casting directors
in New York. You may think
I'm just some backwater hack
... No, no, no,
go directly to New York,
do not pass Go, collect
millions and *millions* of
dollars,
I know whereof I speak.
JEN.
I agree.
NATHANIEL.
You are going to make
me look like
Elia fucking Kazan.

HAKIJA.
Who's that?

NATHANIEL.
Oh, ship me straight
to the old

doesn't want to know.
Too painful.
That's what's so modern.

CHRISTMAS.
But still ... I mean ...
The Fate
thing ... Wh – ?

PAOLA.
Let it goooo, we're all fated.
You're fated to be tall, cute,
you're fated to be gay,
you're –

CHRISTMAS.
You can tell?

PAOLA.
I'm sorry, I just assumed ...

CHRISTMAS.
No, it's okay.

actors home.
Some people *have*
to be actors, and
you're one, you're the
only one of them in this
room.   Probably. *(To JEN.)*
No offense, plus, you
went to Yale, you don't
need introductions.

HAKIJA.
You went to Yale?
FANNY.
Nate?

NATHANIEL.
Hm-hm?

JEN.	CHRISTMAS.	FANNY.
Wow.	I'm out!	I'm curious what made
....	I'm proud!	you decide to stay in
....	I'm just curious	Cambridge rather than
That was	how you ...	starting a company in,
nice.	Never mind.	I don't know,
....		New York or in some
		other city, it seems like
		this town is sort of –

JEN.
You have an amazing smile.
... ...
It's like ... I don't know ... a lamp coming on.

PAOLA.
No, no, I mean, how does ... any[one] ... ?
... .
(To Nathaniel.)
What?

NATHANIEL.
Oh. Yeah ...
(Pause.)
Well, yeah,
you should ask ...

NATHANIEL.
She asked why we decided to stay in Cambridge, rather than ...
JEN. (To HAKIJA, about to ask something.)
But –

PAOLA.
Oh. You can tell her.

PAOLA.
(To CHRISTMAS.)
Not because you're femmy or anything, it's the way you look at people according to gender.

CHRISTMAS.
Sure. But ... can I ask you
–   something else? / On a –

NATHANIEL.
Paola was diagnosed HIV [positive] right after we got married and ...
          (Jen and Hakija
I'm negative.
          overhear the
and she, we,   HIV
          conversa-
were both sick   tion,
          stopping
of New York   them

PAOLA.
Sure.

CHRISTMAS.
And you can tell me honestly:
Do I seem really
fake as the Messenger?

PAOLA.
No.

CHRISTMAS.
Really?

PAOLA.
Not to me. But it's, well,
it's between you and Nate.

CHRISTMAS.
Sure.

PAOLA. *(Pulling him away from NATHANIEL.)*
But how have the two ... I mean,
How have you been approaching
it? Don't tell him I asked you.

CHRISTMAS.
Of course not. Well, *Nate*

short.)
and the L.A.
ratrace, we
thought
it would be
better for our
health, we got
out of the
look – competition –
let our
union member-
ships expire ...

FANNY.
Sure.

NATHANIEL.
Very liberating.

JEN. *(To Hak, re: Nate and Paola.)*
Wow.

NATHANIEL.
It's good to have your
whole life snatched out
from under you every
few years.
FANNY.
Uh-huh.

thinks that –
– which, maybe if someone
else was
playing it might be
a great choice, /
but *on me feels* –

NATHANIEL.
It is! And very few people
get to have that – without it
destroying them, I mean –

FANNY.
Yeah.

*(JEN touches FANNY's back, and FANNY instantly recoils,
    pulling away from her touch.)*

JEN.
Fanny doesn't like
me talking to you.

HAKIJA.
No?

JEN.
She thinks you're
kind of, well,
dangerous.

HAKIJA.
I am.

CHRISTMAS.
Nate says I have
to find a way, like, a
need to unburden
myself or
something, that it's
a life-threatening
trauma this guy
faces because of
what he sees, but …

PAOLA.
What if … … …
… … … …

NATHANIEL.
I'm quite – I
believe that, I'm
not being coy and
ironic, it's
made me
Appreciate
everything –

FANNY.
Yes.

NATHANIEL.
That's actually the
one way… IF you
were going, I were
going to take a
particular, you
know, slant on the
play – I

JEN.
Oh? Really? ...
How
so?

HAKIJA.
I am the plague.
I am the plague.
I am the plague.
Remember?

JEN.
Why does everyone
keep moving?
Do I smell?

HAKIJA.
Yes.
You smell good.

JEN.
Oh.
Good.

*(Again, JEN allows
silence to fill up*

Think about
what it's like
to be present
at an event
like that, John
Lennon's murder
or Hinckley
shooting ...to
witness a
shared,
a national
tragedy –

...something
everyone sees on the
TV? [I mean——]

CHRISTMAS.
YES! What a great
idea!
YES!

Why didn't I think of
that?

PAOLA.
Sh. See if Nate ...

I mean, it's not my
place. But ...
important question:

mean, that would
be the one I'd –
and I'm *not*
going to do that, I
hate that in
produc-
tions where you
can see the god-
damn point
of view of
the director
like handprints
from a blind
Person feeling
their way around
the set after
they've fallen into
paint: you see?,
it's all about the
"Riddle of Human
Identity" – who
are we? It's all
about repression,
right????, and the
Freudians
all leap up and
cheer, or it's about
rootlessness, the
homeless!
Oedipus, poor
thing,
is thrust out of his

between her and
HAK; perhaps she
looks away or their
knees touch.)

You mind? Do you
sleep with women
too?

warm home as an
infant no less and
then he's thrust
out again, for
good, and blind no
less, as an adult!
Social workers,
take note. And
socialists.

CHRISTMAS.
What is this? First
week of rehearsal,
should I just strip or
something?
PAOLA.
Sure.
CHRISTMAS.
Yes. Sometimes.
PAOLA.
Uh-huh.
FANNY.
How many? In your
whole life.
CHRISTMAS.
Women? Let's see

… … …

… … …

One… and a half.
FANNY.
Ooo, what was that
like, sleeping with
half a woman, I
mean?

JEN.
What makes an
ordinary person
… neighbors,
friends … do
those things …
you said.

HAKIJA.
Greed.

JEN.
Uh-huh.

HAKIJA.
The Serbs got rich
off the slaughter
of Muslims, it's
that simple.
Land, jobs,
factories.

JEN.
What about …
Don't you think, I
mean, Fanny says
the same thing,
people'll do
anything for
money, but—

PAOLA.
Have you
noticed this?
On a related
topic: how
directors are
always saying: "We
must get naked, we
must be unafraid,
expose our deepest
selves" –
Meanwhile,
they sit there fully
clothed, hiding their
own emotional,
hell, their own *real*
erections.

CHRISTMAS.
Of course.
All the time.

PAOLA.
Right?

NATHANIEL. *(Cont.)*
Or it's about the
civilized versus the
bestial, our cultural,
learned behavior in
opposition to the
savage creature
within who must then
be cast out, the
scapegoat, you see!
Tragedy itself, the
word, is based on
this: the goat! Goat
festival, or some
fucking thing, Paola
can tell you.

FANNY.
Tooooo
erections!

HAKIJA.
Milosevic̨ built
himself a palace.

JEN.
Is it only that?

HAKIJA.
What then, the devil?

JEN.
No, but ... Well, the
irrational. What Sophocles
is talking about:
the gods.

HAKIJA.
I am an atheist.

CHRISTMAS.
Erections!

PAOLA.   NATHANIEL.
Anyway.   Erections!

FANNY.
No, I'm listening.

NATHANIEL.
I've finished grinding my ax.

FANNY.
I sort of see what you're saying.

NATHANIEL.
That's just me, you know.

FANNY. Why don't you go Equity? Nate? Paola?
NATE. Oh, A.R.T. is in town, you know.
PAOLA. Oh, Nate, for heaven's sake.
JEN. You must ...
NATE. What?
JEN. ... hate them.
PAOLA. These are your friends!
HAKIJA. Serbs?
NATHANIEL. I ... realize, wh[at] – ?
PAOLA. *(Continuous, over.)* They like you.

(HAKIJA is looking for a book during:)

PAOLA. This is our first production, maybe only
production, we're coming out of sort of a hibernation.

FANNY. Oh, cool.

(HAKIJA has found a book.)

JEN.
What's this?
HAKIJA.
I found this
when I was
preparing
to audition.
From *Ajax*.
"Our Enemies
must be
despised as
ones who
will someday
become
our friends,
and our friends
must be helped,
always, as ones
who may not
always be
our friends."
...
"For most men,
the safety of-

NATHANIEL.
Well, that's true. But I really –
(Sound dropping for:)
– do love working with
students, though, truly, I love
especially being able to help
them with–

PAOLA.
In bed.

NATHANIEL.
Some of the training programs
here are less than great, so
having a positive effect on
their-

PAOLA.
In bed.

NATHANIEL.
Okay, cool it with the –

PAOLA.
I'm being funny.

NATHANIEL.
Yes, well, I'll be the judge of
that.
CHRISTMAS.
I like what you said about TV

JEN/HAKIJA.
--friendship, of love,
will not last."

HAKIJA.
You know it?

JEN.
A lot of students do it for class.
"Everything is brought by time
itself from

JEN/HAKIJA.
Darkness into light."

being our messenger, though.
PAOLA.
Did I say that?

NATHANIEL.
Oh, please.

CHRISTMAS.
It brings all the horrible news.

PAOLA.
Right, well, nothing's
particularly changed since way
back then:

NATHANIEL.
Oh, nothing's changed.

(During the following, HAKIJA and JEN become more intimate, more physical; she goes along with it for a while; perhaps it takes place below the table or in their faces and on their arms, and there is a negotiation, a build, boundaries being breached. FANNY begins to take notice.)

PAOLA. – we still find it deeply gratifying to watch stories and to see human beings struggling and going down in flames.

NATHANIEL. Nothing's changed.

PAOLA. Nate, do you mind if other people actually have thoughts? I mean, unless this is a cult and you are going to be administering the Kool-Aid.

NATHANIEL. Jeese.

PAOLA. I mean, it's gratifying to see people in agony IF you're safely on the sidelines –

FANNY. Yes.

PAOLA.	NATHANIEL.
Somebody tells you about something	Don't encourage her.
awful, why do we thrill to that?	

FANNY.

YES YES YES!

NATHANIEL. To compare the awe these plays must have

CHRISTMAS. Because – I –

PAOLA. It isn't enough he gets to monopolize rehearsal. All of life must be the Nate Townsende Show.

NATHANIEL. *(Over, continuous.)* – inspired and to people who were practically gods themselves to the dead-brained slobs chewing their cuds over the evening news is the kind of specious – What did you … ?

PAOLA. SHUT UP, honey!

(Over the last part of this, JEN has tried to stop HAKIJA from proceeding, and he tries to overcome her; the brief struggle or misunderstanding ends with her suddenly standing or shoving him away – knocking over a glass or a chair, something physical, loud. FANNY is already out of her chair, moving to JEN.)

JEN. Christ. I'm sorry, it's not you –

FANNY. Well, time to go learn our lines.

HAKIJA.	CHRISTMAS.
Sorry.	No!

JEN. No. No. Okay, everybody, sorry.

PAOLA. To be continued.

CHRISTMAS. Yes. Thank you.

PAOLA. Remind me.

CHRISTMAS. I will. But we just got here!

PAOLA. Which way are you going? I'll drop you.

NATHANIEL. I haven't finished my drink.

PAOLA. Stay. Drink. Talk. I'm fine. And if you keep ordering and they keep bringing before –

NATHANIEL.

Hak?

HAKIJA. *(To NATHANIEL.)* I'll stay. One more.

CHRISTMAS. I'm staying.

PAOLA.

...you finish the last one, you can keep saying that: "I haven't finished my drink!"

FANNY. The men it is!

CHRISTMAS. Night!

FANNY. See you tomorrow.

NATHANIEL.

No, I can't, I shouldn't.

PAOLA. You're sure?

NATHANIEL. Good night everyone.

CHRISTMAS. Ohhhhhh.

PAOLA. You don't have to for me.

NATHANIEL. We have a big day tomorrow. Another night. Okay?

CHRISTMAS. You going too?

HAKIJA. One more.

PAOLA. Good night everyone.

NATHANIEL. Night. Good work everybody. See you in

the morning. Unless you all want to come up to our place.

PAOLA. If you're going to stay up –

NATHANIEL. Oh, right – All right.

PAOLA. That was the point of my leaving.

NATHANIEL. Yes / yes.

PAOLA. I want to sleep.

NATHANIEL. Of course.

PAOLA. It's fine.

NATHANIEL. No, no, we should. Sleep. G'night.

(All exit but HAKIJA and CHRISTMAS. Pause.)

CHRISTMAS. That was weird. *(Short pause.)* What happened? ... What do you think? Did something ... I thought everybody was having a good time. *(Pause)* What did it ... What did it seem like to you? *(Pause)* Those two.

HAKIJA. Fear.

CHRISTMAS. Fear?

HAKIJA. That's what it seemed like.

CHRISTMAS. Of? ... That you would ... talk about things in Yugoslavia, maybe? Or ...

HAKIJA. Just fear.

CHRISTMAS. Oh. Fear ... Of ...

HAKIJA. Just ...

CHRISTMAS. Oh. But ... Okay. Fear of what though? Sex? Or ... ? *(Pause)* Oh, I see, if you say what kind then it's not just fear. *(Pause)* So ... *(Pause)* Fear. *(Pause)* You ... think she's hot? Jen. *(Short pause.)* What? Okay, mystery, right. Okay. Forgot. *(Silence)* To mystery. And ... fear. *(Short pause.)* And pity. *(Silence.)* Terror and pity. *(Pause.)* So what was it like? ... The war?

(End of Act One.)

ACT II

Scene 1

JEN. *(To us; she holds up HAKIJA'S book.)*
Ajax:
"Everything is brought by time itself
From darkness into light
Then consigned once more to night,
Nothing so catastrophic
That man can trust it never to come to pass,
No promise, nor force of will,
No edifice so fierce, so high,
It cannot come down upon our heads.
We must learn to yield to the gods."
I don't believe that.

Scene 2

(Rehearsal. All six.)

    PAOLA.
"Haughtiness,"
    FANNY.
" – pride,"
    PAOLA & FANNY.
" – and – "

75

            PAOLA.
"– violence – "
            FANNY.
" – breed – "
            PAOLA & FANNY.
" – tyranny; the – "
            PAOLA.
" – Tyrant – "
            FANNY.
" – means to – "
            PAOLA.
May [I]?
            NATHANIEL. Keep going, please.
            PAOLA.
" – cli/mb – "
            FANNY.
" – climb to – "
            PAOLA & FANNY.
" – heights – "
            PAOLA.
"— belonging to the – "
            PAOLA & FANNY.
" – Gods – "
            FANNY.
"May the – "
            PAOLA & FANNY.
"—Gods – "
            PAOLA.
" – bring him to – "
            PAOLA & FANNY.
" – ruin – "

　　　　FANNY.
" – cast him – "
　　　　PAOLA & FANNY.
" – down – "
　　　　PAOLA.
" – tear him – "
　　　　PAOLA & FANNY.
" – apart – "
　　　　FANNY.
" – reward his – "
　　　　PAOLA & FANNY.
" – hubris – "
　　　　NATHANIEL. People.
　　　　FANNY.
" – with – " Go on?
　　　　NATHANIEL. Please.
　　　　FANNY.
" – with – "
　　　　PAOLA.
" – no – "
　　　　PAOLA & FANNY.
" – profit – "
　　　　PAOLA.
" – whatsoever: break the – "
　　　　PAOLA & FANNY.
" – Tyrant's neck,"
　　　　FANNY.
That's just me. "Neck. Make him – "
　　　　PAOLA & FANNY.
" – untouchable."
　　　　PAOLA.
"If the –"

PAOLA & FANNY.

" – Gods – "

FANNY.

" – allow the – "

PAOLA & FANNY.

" – Tyrant – "

PAOLA.

" – to go –"

PAOLA & FANNY.

" – free – "

FANNY.

"I re[fuse] – "

NATHANIEL. It won't be as funny when strangers have paid money and you look completely bereft of talent.

FANNY.

"I – " Ha ha –

PAOLA.

" – refuse to celebrate in their honor."

FANNY. *(Catching up.)* " – refuse to celebrate in their honor." Ooo, that was kind of cool.

PAOLA. When are we allowed to ask questions?

NATHANIEL. Yes? Yes, ask, now, please, perfect timing.

PAOLA. First of all – well, why did you change it from "dance" to "celebrate."

NATHANIEL. You tell me.

FANNY. *You tell me.*

NATHANIEL. Fanny.

FANNY. Because we're not dancing.

NATHANIEL. That would be one reason.

PAOLA. But it's a *famous,* famous line: the Chorus sang and danced, in dialect no less –

NATHANIEL. I'm per—

PAOLA. – and now they are saying "We won't dance anymore if this whole thing – this whole Dionysian theatrical annual celebration is for naught."

NATHANIEL. Yes?

PAOLA. Well –

NATHANIEL. Your other question?

PAOLA. If we're not going to— … Oh never mind.

NATHANIEL. Go on.

PAOLA. I forget now – Oh. Breaking it up that way creates a kind of expectedness –

NATHANIEL. That's right.

PAOLA. – that could be construed as kind of – …

NATHANIEL. Of?

PAOLA. Unintentionally –

NATHANIEL. Comic? Only if we do it badly.

PAOLA. Oh, I see, the onus is entirely on us, then.

NATHANIEL. That's correct.

PAOLA. Well, if this onus is entirely on me, then I'm – us –

FANNY. Thank you.

PAOLA. I'm going to ask the unaskable.

NATHANIEL. Shoot.

PAOLA. Why are there only two of us? Two elders? In all of Thebes. It has to mean something if we're going to do that. I mean, is everyone else dead from the plague?

NATHANIEL. Okay.

PAOLA. No, not okay: what are you intending? Why two?

NATHANIEL. Fanny?

FANNY. Because the director is a sadist?

NATHANIEL. Why else?

FANNY. Beeeecause you want us to find a way to represent many people?

NATHANIEL. Go on.

FANNY. Beeeececause the Elders are of two minds at all times, their thoughts go back and forth.

NATHANIEL. Okay.

PAOLA. Then it isn't broken up properly.

NATHANIEL. Then break it up another way.

PAOLA. Don't be that way.

NATHANIEL. I'm not being –

FANNY. Okay, we will.

NATHANIEL. Okay, until we receive that, let's take it from the second stasimon: "Fate moves ... " whatever the ... bloody hell –

FANNY. Is that true they sang and danced these in dialect?

PAOLA. In masks and fancy shoes. It would be as if we performed with Appalachian accents and ukeleles.

FANNY. In high heels. Basic[ally]—

NATHANIEL. For fate moves swift.

PAOLA. And it's an ode, not a stasimon.

JEN.	FANNY. *(Sound lowered.)*
Hey. *(Pause.)*	"Whoever committed this bloody
You okay? ...	crime had better fly from here for –
"	
... ...	
	PAOLA & FANNY.
	" – *fate* moves swift – "
	FANNY.
JEN.	" – with – "

What's up?

(Pause.)
JEN.
You guys stay
late?
(Pause.)

JEN.
Christmas?
....
CHRISTMAS.
He told me
horrible things.

JEN.
Hak? ... Like ... ?

CHRISTMAS.
It's kind of ...

JEN.
You don't have
to tell me.
CHRISTMAS.
No, it's really
upsetting ...

JEN.
Oh. Well ... If ...

PAOLA & FANNY.
" – fire – "
FANNY.
" – and – "

PAOLA & FANNY.
" – light – "
FANNY.
"I don't know what to think –
Oedipus? The killer?"
PAOLA.
"What motive would he have?"

FANNY.
"I would never find fault with our
Tyrant who saved the city, banished
the Sphinx. Never will I condemn him."

PAOLA:
Before – I'm sorry – Before ... Nate?
You use Tyrant to mean what it
means to us, and now you use it as the
Greeks meant it.
NATHANIEL.
Yes.

FANNY.
What – ? I'm –

PAOLA.
Well, how is the audience to – ?

CHRISTMAS.
He saw
his whole
family
murdered.
He was
the only
only one
of the
whole
village to
survive
His mother
was shot
in the back,
right in front
of him. They
made his
father and
brother dance
on the edge
of a bridge
and stuffed
pork in their
mouths and
then pushed
them over
the edge.
(Pause.)
Their
heads
washed

NATHANIEL.
They're *kelp*, no matter how much
you explain, how clear you are, they
will still be kelp.

FANNY.
I don't understand what it meant to
the Greeks.

NATHANIEL.
Someone not born King.

PAOLA.
A king who is – Yes, chosen.

FANNY.
And what is kelp, why kelp?

NATHANIEL.
Bottom of the ocean, no light, waving
their insensate tendrils: you have to
shine an awfully bright beam down
there to even reach them at all,
god knows what they perceive:
kelp. Okay, again from, ummm—
Anywhere.

PAOLA.
"What motive would he have?"

up in
a trash
bag down
the river
in another
town. I
mean,
who would,
what kind
of person
would
tell you
that? ...
You know?
... Your own
father? ...

FANNY.
"I would never find fault with
our Tyrant –

PAOLA.
Me, either.

… … …

… … ..

– whoooo saved the city,
banished the Sphinx. Never
will I condemn him."

PAOLA.
Me, either.

NATHANIEL.
"Citizens, is this true?
What I hear?.

PAOLA.
Oh sure.

… … …

Oedipus has
accused me of
conspiring with the Soothsayer?"
FANNY.
"It is, I fear."

… … …

PAOLA.

"Here he is now!"

Say,
here he is.

HAKIJA.
"You! Did you or did you not tell me
to send for that middlesex mumbler,
your little prophet for hire!"
Why Middlesex?

NATHANIEL. Good question. Why middlesexed?

CHRISTMAS. Hm? Me?

NATHANIEL. Why "middlesex?"

CHRISTMAS. I'm sorry, what?

NATHANIEL. Oedipus calls Teiresias "middlesexed."

Why?

CHRISTMAS. Beeeeeecause he's overwrought?

NATHANIEL. Why else?

CHRISTMAS. Because he's a homophobe?

NATHANIEL. Do your research. *(To HAKIJA, voice low.)* He's middlesexed –

CHRISTMAS. Oh, you'll tell him, but I have to do my research.

PAOLA. Because Seers were often hermaphrodites, that's why.	NATHANIEL. Go on.

HAKIJA. "Did you think I would not defend myself? Did you think me such an imbecile?"

NATHANIEL. "Am I allowed to answer these charges?"

(PAOLA gestures for FANNY to follow her to a quiet place.)	HAKIJA. "No! *(Sound dropping?)* You're too good."
PAOLA. What if we were to …	
	NATHANIEL. You're upstaging yourself. *(To PAOLA.)* SH! *(To HAKIJA.)* You have your back to the audience.
	HAKIJA. I don't care.
CHRISTMAS. They had camps … whole rape camps ... A friend's sister was videotaped being raped ... and they ...mutilated her	NATHANIEL. I do.
	HAKIJA. I can act with my back, can't I? We'll see

and kept the camera
running. Killed her.
On tape. He saw it
... Who – ? What kind
of a person would
show you that?
... They beat the men
with sledgehammers
... to death. In public ...
They dragged the, some
professor he knew,
grew up with, somebody
else he knew, tied
the guy to the
back of a
car and
dragged him
until he was
just ... bones
and ... tendons
... *(Pause.)* It's
so horrible.
(Pause.)
People are
so horrible.

JEN.
It's okay, babe.

CHRISTMAS.
Oh ... Nate is
so mean to me.

it on your
face. *(Returns to play.)*
"When Laius
disappeared, was
your prophet in
business then?"

NATHANIEL.
"Yes, and equally respected.

HAKIJA.
"Did he mention me then?

NATHANIEL.
"Not that I'm aware."

HAKIJA.
"Only now he accuses me."

NATHANIEL.
"Be reasonable. Do you, my sister,
and I not rule together? Why would I
risk such foolishness when I already
have the power anyone might seek? If
you don't believe me, go to Delphi,
but don't judge me based on
supposition. Take the time, for time is
the great teacher –" Elders?
PAOLA & FANNY.
"He speaks wisely: quick tempers lead
to quick ends."

HAKIJA.
"If I don't move swiftly, I'll be
swiftly undone."

(Pause.)

JEN.
... Nate?

CHRISTMAS.
I'm ... Oh
god ...
I'm so in
love with
him ...
I'm sorry. I can't.

NATHANIEL.
"Do you mean to banish me?"

HAKIJA.
"I mean to kill you, sir."

NATHANIEL.
"Have you lost your mind?"

JEN.
Shhhhh.
Shhhhh.

PAOLA/FANNY.
"Stop! Jocasta comes! Listen to
reason!"

CHRISTMAS.
Go. I'm fine, it's fine.

NATHANIEL.
... Jo/casta [comes] –- !

JEN.
"You should be ashamed to have this private squabble with
the city in despair – Get inside, both of you!"

NATHANIEL.
"Sister, he wants me executed."

HAKIJA.
"With good reason."

NATHANIEL.
"May the gods take me if I am guilty as charged."

JEN.
"Trust him, please, he swears to the gods, for my sake, and all
those standing here."

FANNY.
I love being a crowd.
    HAKIJA.
"But he accused me of murdering Laius!"
    JEN.
"He knew this himself or learned it somehow?"
    HAKIJA.
"He put the profiteering prophet up to it so he could appear
free of guilt."
    NATHANIEL.

It's really hard to invest–	FANNY.
in anything if you're both	Sorry.
making cracks and whispering	... ...
... ...	Sorry. PAOLA.
Jen.	Sorry.

    JEN. Yeah.
    NATHANIEL. It's about him.
    JEN. Still.
    NATHANIEL. It's always about him.
    JEN . No, I –
    NATHANIEL. It's always about the other person.
    JEN. I understand.
    NATHANIEL. Understanding is the booby prize. Stop
him, stop Creon, get them inside, don't feel sorry for yourself.
    JEN. I wasn't [trying to] – That isn't what I was trying to
[play] –
    NATHANIEL. If crying were acting, my great aunt
Harriet would be Duse. Okay, let's ... everything okay?
    JEN. He's fine.
    NATHANIEL. Okay your homework ... Should we
break?
    CHRISTMAS. No, I'm listening, I'm fine.

NATHANIEL. ... is ... to look into your own lives ...

FANNY. Noooooo!

NATHANIEL. – and to change the narrative, but by only as much as you need to in order to place yourself at the center of a tragedy. A dramatic tragedy, not "Oh, I got hit by a bus and killed," that's tragic for you and the people who love you ... but not in the sense that we're talking about.

FANNY. What's the diff, Buddha boy? ... You tell me.

CHRISTMAS. ... Me? Oh, fate! Which is not predetermination oh no!, no no!

NATHANIEL. Fate what?

CHRISTMAS. The gods ... I'm sorry, I didn't get a lot of sleep .... the gods' will or designs, I don't know, intersect with the desires of man and man always pays. Right?

NATHANIEL. That's exactly right.

CHRISTMAS. Really?

FANNY. But, but, you know? Okay: I had the same problem with AA, okay? I don't believe in god. I don't believe in a higher power.

NATHANIEL. No? Who will you pray to for help with your acting?

FANNY. So mean.

NATHANIEL. Anyway, that's your homework. Oh – yes – lest you go seeking some cozy little narrative in which your personal flaws, your procrastination or your inability to quit smoking – your *guilt,* primarily – From –you can ... *[Read it.]* Charles what is his name?

PAOLA. Segal. *(Reads)*

" [...] it is precisely by showing Oedipus' life against its earlier success and power that Sophocles defines it as tragic and thus creates the form of the "tragic hero" in Western literature: a figure whose force of personality and integrity—"

NATHANIEL. *Integrity*.

PAOLA.

"—set him *(Or her.)* apart for a special destiny of pain and struggle – "

NATHANIEL. Special destiny.

PAOLA.

" –and enable him to confront that destiny with clarity and courage ... after a difficult journey to self-knowledge."

NATHANIEL. Yes? What would it take, what would you have to change in order for your story to even deserve to be considered tragic? *Self-knowledge*. Ah! NOW I SEE! At last. "T'was blind but now I see." "Time, the–" What the fuck is it?

PAOLA.

"Time, the all-seeing, has found you out against your will."

NATHANIEL.

"Count no man fortunate till he is dead."

CHRISTMAS. Nice.

NATHANIEL. That's your homework.

FANNY. Time the all-seeing is about to find us out.

NATHANIEL. And this is just for you, I don't want you to tell these.

Scene 3

(The bar. All six.)

JEN.
I'm not. I'm not going to sleep with him.

CHRISTMAS.
Movies?!?

FANNY.
Well, I happen to know otherwise.

JEN.
No. You don't shit where you eat.

FANNY.
Should sex be compared to feces?

JEN.
We're working together, it's too soon
to me to for to sleep with anyone –
    FANNY.
You're drunk.

JEN.
– for me to sleep with anyone, I'm
not, much less get involved.

FANNY.
But he's so cute.

JEN.
I know.

FANNY.
I caught you! I don't think he's
cute at all!

JEN.
Yes – you do.

NATHANIEL.
The greatest single
corrupting influence
in the 20th Century.
Look:
The worst century
in the history
of all mankind.
How many
people
were killed by
other people –
Hundreds of millions –
Stalin – Hitler –
Pol Pot –

… … …
What?

PAOLA. *(Into his ear.)*
You seemed so calm
today. You're not … ?

NATHANIEL.
No, I'm not. But
thanks for trusting me.
Milosević – one long
nightmare … And
what do you know?!?
When did movies
start? At the top
Of the self-

FANNY.
No! I think he's a user, and if you're
not careful you're going to be helping
him become a citizen and a movie star
and raising his kids because you think
he's a "winner" so you're hitching
your little wagon to him like you did
with Bart, and he may be a winner,
but that isn't going to stop him from
dumping you for another movie star
and then you'll be right where you are
now except with teeny tiny toddlers,
so you can say goodbye to acting once
and for all.

JEN.
Thank you, Teiresias.

(Pause.)

JEN.
You think he's going to be a
movie star?

FANNY .
I do.

JEN.
Me, too.

FANNY.
A mean movie star.

same century!
have it:
empirical
evidence!

CHRISTMAS.
But –

PAOLA.
Don't even bother –

CHRISTMAS.
– couldn't movies be a
symptom of the disease
rather than the actual /
source?

NATHANIEL.
No! Because they
objectify human beings,
they're literally not
there! They're
shadows of people
doing things from
the past, they can be
dead, and often are.

NATHANIEL.
Of course you do. When people are blown to smithereens in movies they're not real. Onstage, the actors are there, live, right in front of you, it's more dangerous, anything could happen, it's the complete antidote to cynicism.

CHRISTMAS.
Do you hey do you think that's why the Republicans are always trying to cut funding to the arts?

NATHANIEL.
I'm Republican.

CHRISTMAS.
Right.

PAOLA.
Not out of conviction, just to appall as many people as possible in as few words.

CHRISTMAS.
Really, though?

HAKIJA.
I like movies.

JEN.
You don't mean any this.

FANNY.
Now who is it who married the doctor who took all of her hard-earned money and all her years of effort and –

JEN.
Okay, we've covered this.

FANNY.
– who claims to have known deep   down   what   an unscrupulous worm he really was but stayed with him out of some kind of blind desire to fix or be taken [care]–

JEN.
Thank you, thank you very –
FANNY.
I wash my hands of you.

PAOLA. Look, Cap d'Antibes. Nice!

CHRISTMAS. If that's true, even if you were to beg me, I would not ever let you ride my face like a mechanical bull. And that decision is final.

Scene 4

(Rehearsal. All six. This sequence, a montage, takes us to Opening Night.)

CHRISTMAS. "Jocasta's dead: her own hand."
NATHANIEL. Okay. What do you want from them?
CHRISTMAS. Tooooo inform them?
NATHANIEL. That's what you're doing, what do you want from –

PAOLA.	FANNY.
Nate?	We have to show you!

NATHANIEL. We're working.

PAOLA.	FANNY.
Take a look at what we –	Two seconds, sorry, Chris.
Ready?	... ...
Hit it!	And a one two three four!

(PAOLA and FANNY are in sunglasses and high heels, singing a blues version of:)

PAOLA & FANNY.
"Add up all the men – ever lived and ever died!
Add my poor life to theirs and what do you get?
Nothing!
Nothing!

Has there ever been a man whose joy was more than smoke?
A vision born in chaos
Then blown to hell again!
You! Oedipus! Our shining star!
You were high and mighty.
And happy as a clam!
Priceless fame and glory!
And what did it get you?
Nothing!
(What did it get you?)
Nothing!
(Nothing I say!)
A whole lotta nothing!
YESSIR!
Nothing. No! Thing!"

    FANNY. That's as far as we've gotten.

    NATHANIEL. What do you want from them? You describe the scene --

    CHRISTMAS. Oh, from ...

    NATHANIEL.– because youuuuu ... ?

    CHRISTMAS. Ummmm – Tooooo – make them see it?

    NATHANIEL. Yes. Okay.

    CHRISTMAS.

"Jocasta's dead: her own hand.
You weren't there,
you can't – know – ..."

    NATHANIEL. Go ahead.

    CHRISTMAS. Can ... ? I was -- What if when I start relaying what I saw, I'm actually sort of thrilled deep down to have been witness to this hideous thing.

    NATHANIEL. ... I don't ...

    CHRISTMAS. Well, you know how like when you have

really bad news about someone important, it makes you feel important too?

NATHANIEL. Uhhh –

FANNY. Yes! Absolutely.

CHRISTMAS. Like ... um ... the people who are there when some like when a politician gets shot, killed, if you are there, you take on some of the grandeur or ... You become more –

FANNY. That is ... Isn't that true though?

NATHANIEL. It's interesting. I hadn't –

CHRISTMAS. I mean, I know you said he's in shock, really traumatized, but ...

NATHANIEL. Well, try it.

CHRISTMAS. And that's true, too.

NATHANIEL. Sure. Why not? Give it a –

CHRISTMAS. Yes?

NATHANIEL. Paola?

PAOLA. I'm sorry, I wasn't listening. What?

NATHANIEL. Give it a –

CHRISTMAS. Okay. I mean, if it doesn't work ...

NATHANIEL. Yes, absolutely.

CHRISTMAS.

"I was. I was there.

She burst in, a Queen, our Queen,

Now demented and wringing her hair,

Running through doors, running –

Then locks herself in the bedroom,

 crying:

Laius, here is our bed, soiled."

Does – ?

NATHANIEL. It's good, keep going.

CHRISTMAS. Oh, good.

FANNY. I love that. Sorry.
CHRISTMAS.
"You weren't there.
"You can't know how
    horrible it was.
I was. I was there.
She burst in, a Queen, our
Queen,
now demented and wringing her
hair, running through doors,
running– "
    NATHANIEL.
Make me see it.

    CHRISTMAS.
– running, running through
doors,
then locks herself in the
bedroom,
    crying:
"Laius! Here is our bed!
Soiled.
Filthy *soil* bringing forth a
husband by a husband,
And children by a child!
All soiled!
We made love!
Which we does she mean?"
"Then the son, husband,
King, Prince,
raving, stamping up
and down and

JEN.
I wish I could have
known your family.
. . . .
How did such a … being
come about?

*(Pause. Soon they will
begin to make out.)*

JEN.
Could I see your
hometown someday?

*(He shakes his head
"No.")*

JEN.
No?

HAKIJA.
Not with me.

JEN.
You would never go?
"All killed save one."

FANNY.
Why do you stay with
Nate?

bellows:
"A weapon!
Now! Where is she?
Find me that double breeding
ground!
    Where?"
And hurls himself against the
door,
breaking the bolts,
falling to his knees before:
His ... wife ... mother ...
hanging by the neck, twisted.
(Silence.)
He frees her from the noose,
glides her down, removes the
golden pins, fingering them –
Holds them up ... then rams the
long pins into: "Wicked, wicked
eyes!"

NATHANIEL.
It's scarier if you're quiet.
... ...
Almost
inaudible.

CHRISTMAS.
Great.
Very good.
"Wicked, wicked eyes!"

PAOLA.
What a funny question.

FANNY.
No, I know you love him,
but... And he loves you,
but ...

PAOLA.
Nate was very successful
when
we met. he'd just made
Cold Kisses.

FANNY.
He directed that? Nate?

PAOLA.
He had a big
development contract at
Fox, and convinced the
studio to use me in this big
period piece instead of I-
won't-say-who but–

FANNY.
Who who who who who
who who who who?
PAOLA.
Here's a picture of

NATHANIEL.
Yeah..

CHRISTMAS.
"You'll never see,
You'll never know my shame,
Go dark for all time,
Blind to what you should never
have seen!"
Nate? One of the books – I
just – says that Laius cursed
his whole family by stealing
somebody's son and raping him
–

Do you think Oedipus is cursed
because of that?

NATHANIEL.
Sure, life ain't fair, what the
hell.
CHRISTMAS.
"Blind to what you should
  never have known.
"This chant goes up:
 "Loved her, loved her,"
Each time striking
again deep into
his eyes, dripping,
oozing bloody
muck, it's caught in his beard,
"Loved her,
loved her."

what I looked like
before the crixivan
started working its
wonders.

FANNY.
You're still beautiful.

PAOLA.
Oh go on. Anyway, they
make [you]–

FANNY.
You are.

PAOLA.
Thank you.
You have to get a physical
when you're going to be
in a big movie –
FANNY.
Sure.

PAOLA.
-- so we got my blood
results back, blah, blah, the
whole thing fell apart,
Nate's big chance, he
blames me; I got
pneumonia, pretty much
you name it, I got it, we
fled Hollywood, thank god

He falls upon her:
the couple – a coupled
punishment upon
a coupled sin,
such happiness.
Once.
Now:
Catastrophe!
Throw wide the doors, let all
Thebes see the father-killer, the
mother– too rank to say.
"I AM THE PLAGUE!
I AM THE PLAGUE
I AM THE PLAGUE
He is spent – Well – ...

Nate
had a private income, my
mother came out to take
care of me, she blames
Nate
who conveniently started
spiraling downward,
buying
drunks, drugs, sampling
everything; then the
anti-virals came along,
I came along, twelve steps,
you know, then we decided
we'd rather drink, he got
the job at Harvard, but --

NATHANIEL. Okay, Creon time.

CHRISTMAS. I know you're going to fire me at the last minute.

NATHANIEL. You can't get out of it that easily.

JEN. I'm really happy right now.

(HAKIJA kisses JEN'S breast through her blouse; they slip out of sight, down a flight of stairs during:)

PAOLA. ... his confidence was ... Scarily so. I mean, like a little child. And, well, he was hearing voices, for a while. *(Pause.)* No longer, but ... this is his first venture back into the world; it's a much bigger deal than he lets on.

(Short pause.)

FANNY. Didn't you want to play Jocasta?

PAOLA. Oh, god no. I think I've had enough of acting. *(Pause.)* That's all you have to say: after what I told you?

FANNY. I, I don't know what else to –

PAOLA. It's okay.

FANNY. Sorry.

PAOLA. No, I like that you never seem to have a hidden agenda.

FANNY. You mean I'm incapable of censoring myself.

PAOLA. Well, I like that, too. *(Pause.)*

CHRISTMAS. You never ever ever *ONCE* slept with a guy?

NATHANIEL. Okay, once.

CHRISTMAS. Oh, tell me, please? Please?

NATHANIEL. *(Beat)* When Paola and I met, she was absolutely sure I was gay, she still is.

CHRISTMAS. Yeah?

NATHANIEL. Don't ask, anyway, she kept saying, You should try it you should try it, I think she just didn't want to be with one more guy who turned out to be bi-, is my theory, she was testing me, so to finally, I just to shut her up said, Okay, I will prove to you I'm not gay, and there was this admittedly rather hunky guy in the cast, and I went right up to him on closing night and said, my wife thinks you're hot, do you want to sleep with us, and we both had seen him eyeing me, I wasn't taking any chances of being rejected –

CHRISTMAS. I would never reject you.

NATHANIEL. – and the guy says, Sure, and we take eight tabs of ecstasy or whatever and we all hop into ... well, the floor, and sure enough I am completely incapable of getting hard, though this guy works so diligently on me I'm still replacing skin he took off ...

CHRISTMAS. Is that who infected her?

NATHANIEL. ... *Where is everybody?* We're not on break, guys. Jen, Hak?

PAOLA. They're ... I just –

(JEN and HAKIJA appear.)

NATHANIEL. Okay, let's look at that foretelling, what is it, prophecy ...

PAOLA. Anybody want anything?

NATHANIEL. Don't go too far.   *(To JEN.)*   Go. Anytime.

JEN.
Uh ... "Hear me now!
Why should any man fear the Gods if Chance is all there is?"
There is no foretelling, no prophesying anything.
Better to live one's life without fear.
All men – "

NATHANIEL. I'm Oedipus, make me believe—
JEN. Okay.
NATHANIEL.

—change my mind.	JEN.
	Okay.
FANNY.	"Hear me now!"
Why do you think ... ?	Why *(drop in volume.)*
... Is it ... possible that Paola and	should any man fear the
I were the only two complete	Gods if Chance is all
dunder heads left in all	there is? Chance!
of Boston and Cambridge	There is no foretelling,
who were actually willing to	no prophecying
play Elders in	anything ... All
this turkey?	men lie with
	their mothers ...

HAKIJA.
Probably not.

FANNY.
No. So ... Why do you think ...
I mean, Nate's a smart guy,
don't you?
HAKIJA.
Nate?
FANNY.
Right?

HAKIJA.
Sure.

FANNY.
Why would he do such a thing?
HAKIJA.
You tell me.

FANNY.
Because ...
... ...
it's almost impossible.

HAKIJA.
Right.

FANNY.
And ....
... ...

in their dreams ...
Those who give it
no more thought
are the happiest!"

NATHANIEL.
I'm unconvinced.
JEN.
Oh.
Okay.

NATHANIEL.
Me.
It's not about you.

JEN.
"Hear me now.
Why should any
man fear the
Gods if
Chance
is all there
is ... ?
       ...
There is no
foretelling,
no prophecying
anything.
Better to

Ohhhh..

HAKIJA.
What?
FANNY.
Thank you.

HAKIJA.
I didn't do anything.

FANNY.
Oh yes you did.
You're the only other person
around here who's devious enough

to have figured it out.

HAKIJA.
I don't know what you're –

FANNY.
Shut up. I mean, thanks.

PAOLA.
Nate.

NATHANIEL.
Why do you say every line as if you
want me to feel sorry for you? Is

live one's
life without
fear."

NATHANIEL.
Sorry.
... ...
Look, I'm not trying
to drive you crazy ...

NATHANIEL.
You love him.
You
want to save his
life!
... ...
You *fuck* him.
Maybe I'd
believe
it more if you'd
waited until
opening night.
JEN.
What?

JEN.
We haven't –

that what you learned at Yale? I
don't remember that. She is
determined to get what she wants,
which is not my pity.

PAOLA.   JEN.
Nate.   No. Of course.
                                I – know –
                                . . . .
NATHANIEL.   . . . .
Cry all you want, cry   . . . .
Cry –   I'm not crying.
Fine, good, but sooner or later
you are going to have to make these
scenes about the person you are
playing to and not yourself   JEN.
and your exquisite and sensitive feelings ...   I know. I agree.
Good. Because nobody cares how
deep we are, any of us. The only
thing anyone cares about is what people
do and how they do it, not what they feel.
You feel too much.

PAOLA. That's enough –
JEN. It's okay.

NATHANIEL. I care– Do you want to direct the play? I
care what Jocasta wants or how she goes about trying to get it.

JEN. Me, too. *(Pause.)* Me, too. I'll get it.

NATHANIEL. Well, it's getting a little late for promises.

Scene 5

(Opening night. A communal dressing room. All six.)

FANNY. You want to know what my tragedy was?, I know we weren't supposed to tell: Instead of being born who I am in 1972, I'm born in ancient Greece and my name is Medea.

STAGE MANAGER'S VOICE. *(Over the loudspeaker.)* Five minutes, ladies and gentlemen, this is five minutes to places.

FANNY. Oh god, baby Jesus.

CHRISTMAS. This is a pagan play. No Jesus.

JEN.

"We learn to give way. For winter storms step aside for summer, terrible storms tame the sea to calm, and the prison of sleep – "

FANNY. *(Sings)*
"To everything, turn turn turn.

(FANNY starts to whistle; several actors sh! her.)

PAOLA.
No! Whistling!
Spit and turn around three times. Do it! Spit and turn around—

FANNY.
No. I won't.
No. No. Too bad. Bad luck.Tra la. Macbeth, Macbeth, Macbeth, Macbeth!

JEN. *(cont'd)*
" – eventually frees all those jailed within."

NATHANIEL.
Do I look as much like Elmer Fudd in this as I think?

JEN.
"Should we never learn our place or come to wisdom? I for one shall learn ... "

NATHANIEL.
Listen, I want you to concentrate
on what is at stake. Always,
every moment, how high are
the stakes for your character at
each and [every] --
STAGE MANAGER'S VOICE.
Five minutes, ladies and gentlemen.
FANNY.
We did that.
STAGE MANAGER'S VOICE.
I'm sorry, make that places!
FANNY.
Ahh, that was not / five minutes!
STAGE MANAGER'S VOICE.

(PAOLA exits.)   My last call was late. Sorry
FANNY.
Now she tells us that?

JEN. Break a leg.

(She leaves. NATHANIEL exits, chanting "Stakes, stakes, stakes!" ???)

CHRISTMAS. I want everyone to promise to be my friend no matter how many dead whale dicks I suck tonight.

FANNY. I promise. And I hope you do, I hope everyone sucks, so I can stand out in bright relief.

(FANNY and CHRISTMAS exit. HAKIJA closes his eyes;
FANNY returns, sees HAKIJA crosses himself in the
fashion on a Serbian Orthodox Christian.)

FANNY. Blind Tereisias forgot his staff.

(She exits. Pause. Music can be heard through the speakers;
the audience grows quiet. HAKIJA exits. We watch the
empty dressing room as, over the speaker on the wall, we
hear the curtain rise, then:)

HAKIJA'S VOICE.
"My children, why are you here, pleading, bent down?
The city is burdened with moans and incense, intertwined,
I would not trust a messenger, so I've come to hear with my
own ears.
Priest, you speak for them?"
CHRISTMAS' VOICE.
"Our ship, the city of Thebes,
Our city, the ship of Thebes,
Can barely lift her prow from these bloody waves:
Plague dragging our people, drowning them in death.
You saved our city once.
You rid us of the cursed Sphinx
Some say with the help of the gods,
We beseech you, help us once more.
If you don't, you will rule over an empty city."

(Lights go to black, then bump right up again, mercilessly
bright, and we are onstage.)

HAKIJA.

"They said I should kill my father!

But he's dead, deep in the soil,

And here I stand, never laying a hand on him!

Unless he died longing for me.

I am not his killer!"

JEN.

"I told you this."

HAKIJA.

"I was too filled with fear to hear you.

But wait – mustn't I now fear my mother's bed?

JEN.

"Hear me now!

Why should any man fear the Gods if Chance is all there is?

Chance!

There is no foretelling, no prophesying anything.

Better to live one's life without fear.

All men lie with their mothers – in their dreams!

Those who give it no more thought than that are the happiest."

(Jump cut to:)

PAOLA & FANNY.

"Add all the lives of all the generations who have lived and died,

Add to these our own, and still you will come up with nothing.

Has there ever been a mortal whose joy was more than fantasy,

A vision born then snatched into oblivion before you blink?

You, Oedipus, are the shining example!

You stood above all men: your happiness all encompassing.

And now is there a man in greater agony?

More joined forever to suffering, frenzy, panic?
Your life's triumphs ground to nothing—chaos."

(Jump cut to:)

CHRISTMAS.
"I AM THE PLAGUE!
I AM THE PLAGUE!
I AM THE PLAGUE!
He is spent. Well ... you may see for yourselves.
Look: the gates are opening."

(Doors open center where we see the body of JOCASTA; from the shadows steps the blinded OEDIPUS.)

HAKIJA.
Oh... oh... where am I going? Which way does my voice go on that wind - [and] how far have these spirits sprung? Dark - a nightmare dark, some fierce wind stinging me with nothing but evil of my own deeds. The gods brought this bitterness to its conclusion, but the hand that struck me was my own. Drive out the criminal, drive out the plague! I cursed myself with the gods' curse. Time's tragic lesson: no mortal creatures ever win,... all borne out before these eyes unseeing... I don't care what is done to me, I won't see it. Treat me as you would a carcass. And lest you trouble yourselves to think of me, to care at all, recall: My own flesh wanted me dead. And rightly so. I would not have these agonies - pictures of my father, I saw him once, as I killed him, my mother, as we wed, making me, forever, godless by the same seed that made me... If there is anything worse in all the world than that, that too is Oedipus. Look on me, bear witness, I cannot, I see too much

to ever see again. If there were means to cut off my hearing I would. Give me a knife, I'll cut out those membranes as well. Give it to me! Apollo! Look now! I gave you your bidding so you might see how shameful, small, and soiled is man. I did what I came to do and am of no use to anyone. Like these putrid, jellied eyes, smashed eggs... Did they fall? Sweep them away: crushed vermin, stabbed, bloody, blinded in god's name. Hide me! I beg you! Look to it! Let no one see. Kill me, smash me on rocks in some festering brine, wash me away! Don't touch me. No one but I can bear this. No one... not even I... But I... No one. This doom... this shame... it is my own.

(End of "Oedipus Tyrannus".)

Scene 6

(Opening night party.)

FANNY.	CHRISTMAS.
YES!!!	Who was that fucking weirdo in the front row with the sparkly glasses? Who was that fucking weirdo in the front row with the sparkly glasses?

NATHANIEL.

That's why I didn't want to limit it! Yes, all of those interpretations are valid and they're all there, you don't have to pick one over the other – In fact, if you do that, you don't allow the audience to have their own, I mean,

FANNY.
Glasses?
CHRISTMAS.
He was fast asleep.

you have to trust them, audiences
are smarter than we give
them credit for.

PAOLA.
I saw him.

FANNY.
JEN.   The kelp, you mean?
Oh oh oh!
(To HAKIJA.)
Tell them!
Tell the – ! Oh –

CHRISTMAS.
You did?
          PAOLA.
          That was
          my agent.

CHRISTMAS.
No! Really? Oh.

HAKIJA.
What?

FANNY.
JEN.   Christmas gave me an ecstasy,
Your theory! About Oedipus   do you want one?
and the U.S.!

PAOLA.
HAKIJA.   No, *oh, don't give Nate one,*
Oedipus and ... Oh! No.   *please.*
JEN.
Yes. Hak was saying, this was like   FANNY.
weeks ago, that he saw – You say it.   You sure?

HAKIJA. I said that the U.S. reminds me of Oedipus –
you made your place in the world by native wit alone, and
proved you deserve to be number one.

NATHANIEL. That's very interesting.

FANNY. You hate that sort of interpretation.

JEN. No, but. I don't remember that good stuff about
America, though, I thought –

CHRISTMAS.
That's because he knows he's

talking to a Republican.

PAOLA.
St. Paul de Vence.

JEN. Who's a Republican?

(CHRISTMAS points to NATHANIEL.)

JEN. You are not.
CHRISTMAS. Smile!

*(CHRISTMAS takes a photograph of JEN in shock; he will
     continue taking photos.)*

FANNY. Thank you, now I'm blind.

JEN. Well then I'll tell you what he really said. He said
we make ourselves willfully blind to our power, we can't
afford to see that we're the ones making the world unlivable,
we blame everyone and anyone but ourselves, "Oh, they hate
us because we're free, we have a Democracy."

NATHANIEL. And it's true.

JEN.
The rest of the world knows very
well what we've done –

CHRISTMAS.
You were both
really good, I
watched during
all my times
offstage which

NATHANIEL.
Help them time and time and time again,
you mean? At our own expense?

as you know
are frequent.
... ...

JEN.
By being the world's foremost
exporter of weapons?
Can I have another? Thank you.
Republican?

That horrible

FANNY. *(To Hakija.)*
You listen to me, all right? ... Don't
fuck with her. Jen. I'm totally --

HAKIJA.
Don't...?

FANNY. *(Over him, not stopping.)*
Hey. I'm not that drunk, or even drunk.
Yet. So, just because everybody
loves you and I love you, too, I do, I
think you're great, and but I want you
to know that that doesn't mean you
can use her and walk away or some –

HAKIJA.
I think –

FANNY.
No, no, I have more, and you
listen. She's been exploited
before. If you are just hoping
to become a citizen or something,
prove yourself worthy of her, she
is better than the rest of us –

NATHANIEL.
Why is it that
some Americans
can only see evil-
why is it always
the U.S.,
somehow
the rest of the
world, it's world,
it's all these
sweet little
baby deer
and we're
the wolves --
Always.

JEN.
I'm not saying that.

NATHANIEL.
Hear me out. If we didn't
produce weapons and
have such strong defense,
I can promise,
you would be captive
in some Arabian
cave, if they hadn't
already raped you
and fed you to their
camels.
JEN.
Are you a racist too, Nate?

HAKIJA.
I couldn't agree more.

FANNY.
As long as we're clear.
Because, if she weren't so great,
I would have fucked you in a
heartbeat, so there.

CHRISTMAS. *(Shouting)*
Hey!
... ...
Hey everybody!
... ...
Has anybody ever
played Yes or No?
PAOLA.
Yes or No?

PAOLA.
Whoa whoa whoa, party,
everyone!
JEN.
Do you come from a lot of
money or something?

PAOLA.
Scads. Piles. Oodles.
Mountains.
NATHANIEL.
We were comfortable.

JEN.
Only rich people say that:
comfortable.

FANNY.
I think I have.
Is that – ?

CHRISTMAS. Oh, this is so fun!
FANNY. Is that the one – ?
CHRISTMAS. Listen up, everybody, we're going to play this game!
FANNY. Listen!
PAOLA. I hate games.

(All ad lib responses during:)

CHRISTMAS. Okay, all you can do is answer Yes or No. There's no maybe's, no, welllll, no explaining. Somebody starts, asks somebody a question, they say yes or no, and then that person gets to ask anyone else a question. But –

NATHANIEL. Are we trying to – ?

CHRISTMAS. To?

NATHANIEL. Guess something?

CHRISTMAS. No no no!

NATHANIEL. What's – ?

CHRISTMAS. Oh, listen, the most important thing, and we have to swear: Nothing that's said ever leaves this room. You can't play if you don't promise.

NATHANIEL.
No surer way to guarantee the dissemination of a rumor than to ask for secrecy.

... ...

I swear!

FANNY.
We promise!

CHRISTMAS.
Does everybody swear to keep whatever is said in this room in this room?

PAOLA.
He's got his fingers crossed!

(Ad lib: "Yes, I promise," "We swear! etc.)

NATHANIEL. All right, all right, I swear.

CHRISTMAS. Okay, who wants to go first?, me! This is just to skip to the chase, because usually everybody starts with these nice, bland questions and it takes a while till everybody gets bored enough to start asking really interesting questions so I thought I'd start.

FANNY. Just ask the question!

CHRISTMAS. Nate: When you called, said Merry Christmas, that time, to me, were you saying that I was a big girl and too slight onstage like Mary M-A-R-Y?

NATHANIEL. What?

CHRISTMAS. Were you saying M-A-R-Y Christmas?

NATHANIEL. No. Jesus. All this time. you've been ... ?

CHRISTMAS. Okay. Thank you. It's all right. Just a question.

NATHANIEL. Awwww. Dooo – oh... ??? *(To JEN.)* Did you vote in the last election?

JEN.	PAOLA.
Ummm –	Like a dog
	with a bone.
FANNY.	... ...
Tell the truth.	You!

JEN. I'm thinking, I'm thinking. When was the last election? No.

NATHANIEL. Ah-ha! Armchair radical.

JEN. I confess, yes. You're right. Are ... *(To HAKIJA)* ... you really in love with me?

HAKIJA. Yes.

CHRISTMAS.	
Awwwwww, how	PAOLA.
sweet is that?	No hesitation, how about that?

NATHANIEL. Well, what is he gonna say in front of all of us?

CHRISTMAS. Well, does that mean you were saying I'm a big girl?

HAKIJA. *(To JEN.)*

Did you know –	FANNY.
... ...	Nobody's asked me a
Did you know your friend Fanny	single question!
was going to come to me tonight	
and warn me not to hurt you –	

JEN. She did?

HAKIJA. Did you put her up to it?

JEN. She did?

CHRISTMAS. Yes or no.

JEN. Really?

CHRISTMAS. Guess that's a no.

JEN. Seriously?

FANNY.

Yes. So, Nate,   JEN.

diiid you really –   That wasn't my question.

Too bad, you asked a question,

did you cast only two elders so Paola

would be so busy figuring out a way to

solve the problem she wouldn't be able

to become a back seat director?

NATHANIEL.   PAOLA.

Did she tell you that?   *What?!*

FANNY. Yes or no.

NATHANIEL. Yes. Did you ... come up with that?

FANNY. No. Just a guess –

PAOLA. Wait wait wait –

NATHANIEL. It's not your turn.

FANNY. Uhhh, Hak – Do atheist Muslims usually cross themselves like Christians?

HAKIJA. Sometimes – I –

FANNY.

Yes or no   PAOLA.   HAKIJA.   NATHANIEL.

I said usually.   Yes, I   I'm kidding!   Back seat

                  suppose.   director ...

CHRISTMAS. They do?

HAKIJA. No. Not usually.

FANNY. Before the show, he did. "Father, Son and Holy Ghost." I caught you!

PAOLA.

Any superstition will do,   FANNY.

at that point.   Closet Christian.

HAKIJA. Paola, do you think that Nate knows [you]– No, no, I can't.

FANNY. Too late, you have to say it.

HAKIJA. No.

PAOLA. Go ahead, I what?

CHRISTMAS. Ask something else.

NATHANIEL. No, go ahead.

CHRISTMAS. It's just a game, guys, this isn't approved by the American Psychiatric Association, okay?

NATHANIEL. Ask your question.

HAKIJA. Does Nate know you were working with many of the actors in secret?

PAOLA.

Oh, come on – No.	NATHANIEL.
That's like "Why do you beat	Yes or no?
your wife?" I did a little coaching.	
I did some coaching.	

NATHANIEL. Yes. Is the answer.

PAOLA. Yes. *(Pause.)* You're making it sound like … a big deal.

NATHANIEL.

I'll take one of those ecstasies.	PAOLA.
Thank you.	No.
	… … …
CHRISTMAS.	… … …
Really?	Honey, please –
Well, I don't …	… … …
	That's ridiculous –
NATHANIEL.	… … …
It's not addictive.	Punish me –
And I don't need a	not yourself.
coach. Yes. Thanks	
for the offer. It'll be fine.	

CHRISTMAS. Let's all take off our clothes or play another game at least.

PAOLA. You don't really care that I helped people, do you? It wasn't– directing, I wasn't–

NATHANIEL. No. Would you be even capable of seeing my casting two people as the chorus as a compliment, the idea that you could actually solve that, and brilliantly, *if* it were true I done that?

	CHRISTMAS.
PAOLA.	If? You keep doing that!
Yyyyyes	
and	FANNY.
no.	Shhh.
FANNY.	CHRISTMAS.
Yes or no.	Seriously.

PAOLA. What are you, the game police? No. Did you?

NATHANIEL. No. Jen: would, let's see, being a huge, highly-paid, much admired, award winning, healthy, slim, ever-young world-traveling movie star make you happier than having a loving home with a husband who genuinely adored you and a beautiful, healthy child to call your own?

JEN.

No.

FANNY.	CHRISTMAS.
Oooooo.	I believe her.
	… … I want
HAKIJA.	a child … …
Jen's turn …	… … …
	God.

JEN.

Um …

PAOLA. I'm sorry, honey.

NATHANIEL. I'm fine.

PAOLA. All right. *(Pause.)* Ask if –

FANNY. Let her do it.
PAOLA. All right.

                              JEN.
(Pause.)   I'm thinking ...

CHRISTMAS. Anything. Off the top of your head.
                              HAKIJA. *(Mouthed to JEN who
                              looks at him.)*
(Pause.)   What?

NATHANIEL. Don't even think about it, just ...

(Pause.)

FANNY. Anything.
PAOLA. Let her do it!

*(FANNY sticks out her tongue; PAOLA sticks out her tongue;
the two kiss.)*

Scene 7

JEN. *(To us.)* Nate was good for his word; in no time at
all Hak found an agent, changed his name and abandoned
economics for New York. Fanny and Paola ... fall in love.
They're both sober and live in Northampton where they run a
ski shop in winter and a landscape business in the summer;
they're adopting a Chinese baby. Christmas works for them
and rents an apartment in their house. Nate and Paola are no
longer friends. He has returned to New York and found work
directing ... a soap opera. He lives down the hall and is our
closest friend.

(The sound of a baby crying.)

JEN. That's Naomi. She's seven months and three days old. Hak and I are discussing maybe having one more.

(Pause; the baby continues crying.)

JEN. Oh, I let her cry; I know when she's hungry or needs to be changed, and she usually stops in a minute or two. I know some people disagree with that, but a) I'm not some people, b) she's one of the happiest and easiest babies I've ever known, and c) fuck them with their unsolicited opinions.

(The baby has stopped crying.)

JEN. See? *(Beat.)* Hak has a scene today and tomorrow with Robert de Niro in an independent film about – Guess what! – the Mafia! Life is nothing if not predictable. If you know how to read all the clues and take the time to put them together. I was never one to do my homework ...

(Intercom buzzes. She moves to it; into the intercom:)

JEN. Yes?

CHRISTMAS. Hey, Jen, it's Chris ... Christmas? And – Fanny and Paola?
JEN. Oh, hiiiiii! Come on in. My god. *(She buzzes them in. She opens the door.)* Oh my god.
FANNY. Surprise.
JEN. I can't believe it. The Messenger, the Prophet, the Elders!

(CHRISTMAS, PAOLA and FANNY enter the apartment; they are in winter garb.)

JEN. How are you? What a treat, wow.
CHRISTMAS. Is Hak here?
JEN. No, he's working. Take off your coats.
PAOLA. Hey, baby.
JEN. He'll be sorry to miss you, what's going on?
FANNY. We're Christmas shopping.
CHRISTMAS. I said you'd be home, we took a chance.
JEN. I'm glad.
CHRISTMAS. You look great.
JEN.

So do you, all of you, my god.	CHRISTMAS.
Your hair!	Where's all that
	fat you're
PAOLA.	supposed
I know.	have
	after having a
	baby?
JEN.	
You look fantastic.	
You do. Oh.	PAOLA.
All of you.	Is she, is she asleep?
You can look. Go on in.	

(PAOLA and CHRISTMAS exit.)

FANNY. How are you?
JEN. I'm good. Do you want to see?
FANNY. I don't want to wake her.
JEN. You won't.

(FANNY exits as CHRISTMAS re-appears.)

JEN. Are you well?

CHRISTMAS. It's good to see you.

JEN. Oh, you, too. Is everything ... ? I mean.

CHRISTMAS. We're fine, we're good.

JEN. I'm sorry Hak isn't here.

(Pause.)

CHRISTMAS. Great place.

JEN. Oh, I forgot you hadn't seen it.

CHRISTMAS. Fabulous. Really. I, hey, is that your voice on the mayonnaise commercial?

JEN. It is.

CHRISTMAS. I knew it! I hear you a lot, I think.

JEN. Yeah, that's been good. And I can take Naomi with me, usually, sometimes I get a sitter. Nate, actually.

CHRISTMAS. Townsende?

JEN. He lives down the hall.

CHRISTMAS. Oh my god, don't tell ...

JEN. I won't. I can make a pot of coffee.

CHRISTMAS. I'm good. Thanks.

JEN. So ... god ... well, do you miss it? Acting?

CHRISTMAS. Oh, no, I, you know?, always felt like I was standing up there in a sundress with a big wet lollipop. I wanted to ... act, really act, be active the world in ways that would make it better or at least try to.

JEN.	
Great. That's	CHRISTMAS.
wonderful.	Yeah.

(PAOLA and FANNY re-enter.)

PAOLA. Oh my god what?

CHRISTMAS. What?

PAOLA. Oh, please. Oh my god what? [I heard someone say ...]

JEN. Nate lives right down the hall. Two apartments over.

PAOLA. I'm gonna be sick.

JEN. I'm sorry. I would have told you if you'd called.

PAOLA. I don't want to know how he is unless he's really awful.

JEN. Okay. Fair enough.

PAOLA. He's not?

FANNY.

... She looks so much like you.   CHRISTMAS. *(To PAOLA)*
                                    Breathe.

JEN. You think? I can only see Hak. Around the mouth? *(Pause.)* Can I get you anything? Tea? Coffee? No? Are you drinking?

CHRISTMAS. Not officially.

JEN. Ah ha. Oh, he's going to be heartbroken he missed you, you're welcome to hang around. *(Pause.)* Did you see him on Law and Order? His accent's almost gone, he's been working with a dialect coach. He's shooting today and tomorrow with Robert De Niro, a feature. *(Pause.)* Okay, what's going on?

FANNY. We missed you.

CHRISTMAS. Nothing.

(Short pause.)

JEN. Okay.

PAOLA. Okay, you can tell me, what's he doing?

JEN. Nate? He's subbing on a soap.

PAOLA. Which?

JEN. Betrayals.

PAOLA. Oh good.

JEN. Why?

PAOLA. It stinks. Serves him right.

JEN. Oh. You're right it does. But ... well.

PAOLA. Is he seeing anyone?

JEN. We see him most nights.

PAOLA. Oh, so he's seeing you. Are you all having sex?

JEN. He's straight.

PAOLA. I'll be the judge of that, thank you. I know he thinks I left him because of Fanny, but that isn't why. I left him because I had to take care of him and I was the one who was sick.

JEN. ... Uh-huh.

PAOLA. And at some point during our play, I started to feel –

JEN. You don't have to justify yourself.

PAOLA. Maybe I do. I don't care how fantastic the production was ultimately, rehearsing should be about cooperation, collaboration –

JEN. Uh-huh.

PAOLA. – not dictatorship. And all that process bullshit.

JEN. I –

PAOLA. He scapegoated you!

JEN. Well –

PAOLA. Terribly. And look how many of us quit acting after that production, half!

JEN. I don't – He helped me in the part, I felt; he brought Hak and me together, so ... I have, obviously, very different feelings. *(Silence.)* I'm sorry it was so hard.

PAOLA. I lucked out. I'm not complaining. *(Pause.)*

JEN. Why don't you stay for dinner? I'll send out ...

CHRISTMAS. Well, no, we wanted to ...

JEN. Are you sure? Oh. What?

CHRISTMAS. See you, you know, just you.

JEN. Oh. Why?

CHRISTMAS. Well ...

JEN. Something's wrong. Isn't it?

(PAOLA, FANNY and CHRISTMAS look at one another.)

JEN. What?

PAOLA. We weren't sure you'd be alone.

CHRISTMAS. We didn't want to just call you up or send a letter.

JEN. All right.

FANNY. We thought you should have friends with you when ...

JEN. When what?

(Short pause.)

CHRISTMAS. I – ...

JEN. What?

FANNY. We have been seriously debating whether or not we should even do this.

JEN. Do what?

CHRISTMAS. I went to Hak's hometown.

JEN. In Bosnia?

CHRISTMAS. Yes. Through my church, I'm Unitarian now, I got involved in food distribution and ... I went over twice, actually.

JEN. Wow.

CHRISTMAS. The second time I ...

JEN. That's ... [wonderful?]

CHRISTMAS. ... because we all loved him, we were all so close, and he was such an inspiration to all of us – I don't know, I wanted to see his home. Or ...

JEN. Uh-huh.

CHRISTMAS. Everything's been partitioned ...

JEN. Yes.

CHRISTMAS. And but many people are returning. A surprising [number]. The trials, I think, at the Hague –

JEN. Uh-huh.

CHRISTMAS. – are encouraging people, or are going to, anyway ...

JEN. What's it ... ? Tell me.

CHRISTMAS. I asked around about Hak, and told everyone I knew him and ... I got a ... strange ... Everyone said he was dead.

(Short pause.)

JEN. Why?

CHRISTMAS. Well, I said, No, I know him, he's told me all about the town, and I described him, I – and everyone said, No, Hakija looked nothing like that, he was not tall, he and his family were killed on the same day ... *(Pause.)* And I left.

FANNY. We weren't going to do anything.

CHRISTMAS. And ... I took a few names, said I would write. I ... copied a few photos of Hak and sent them over ... I was ... concerned, I don't know.

JEN. Uh-huh.

CHRISTMAS. And everyone I sent them to wrote back, individually, maybe they ... They said the man in the photograph was a Bosnian Serb, from that town, who had participated in the ...

(Pause.)

JEN. I don't –

PAOLA. He'd been part of the massacres. He was particularly –

JEN. Thank you. *(Short pause.)* Yes.

(Pause.)

    CHRISTMAS. You don't want to know?
    FANNY. Everyone said –
    JEN. Thank you. That's ...
    FANNY. – he was one of the ringleaders, one of the most brutal, a rapist.
    JEN. That's enough. *(Pause.)* I wonder if I can get my money back. Do they do that with babies?

(Short pause.)

    CHRISTMAS. I wrote back again and said it couldn't be him. Not possible.

(Silence.)

    FANNY. We were sent ...

(She produces a videotape.)

    CHRISTMAS. I said we shouldn't come.
    FANNY. I'm sorry.
    JEN. Keep it. Take it.

(Pause.)

    FANNY. You can throw it away if you don't – You don't have to look at it.
    JEN. True. Okay. Well. Merry Christmas.
    CHRISTMAS. Should we not have told you – ... ?
    JEN. Don't give it another thought, flee.
    PAOLA. Watch the tape.

JEN. How could I dare to be happy? ... Is that ... ?

FANNY. You know this has nothing to do with that.

JEN. Would you have told him? To his face? If he'd been here. Would you? ... Would you?!

PAOLA. I would.

FANNY. We just didn't want you living with someone who might ...

JEN. Well, I'm sure you're right. Good luck with your new child, I hope she works out -- her father doesn't turn out to be some kind of war criminal, you'll have to --

FANNY. Stop.

(Silence.)

CHRISTMAS. Did you know already?

JEN. ... Goodbye.

CHRISTMAS. Did you?

FANNY. You know that we all love you very much. And I'm --

CHRISTMAS.	JEN.
We do, baby.	Yes.

FANNY. -- concerned about you. That's all.

JEN. Are you going to, what, now, go to the relief agencies, denounce him?

CHRISTMAS. We would never --

JEN. You would never--What are the things you would never?

PAOLA. Watch that fucking tape, do you understand? We're not talking about plays and commercials and Robert de fucking Niro—

FANNY. Honey -- Babe--

PAOLA. -- we're talking about human beings, we're talking about savagery, you fucking little cow, how dare you act all huffy, he should be on trial!

    CHRISTMAS. Come on now.

    PAOLA. You think all this is going under the rug, you fucking little—

(JEN closes the door.)

    PAOLA. Get your hands off, don't be such a fairy, both of you, I'm sick of all the nice nice, these are indecencies, crimes against – !

    FANNY'S VOICE. All right, baby.

    PAOLA'S VOICE. Not all right, NOT.

    FANNY'S VOICE. Okay.

    PAOLA'S VOICE. She should be begging, they both should – God sees! For mercy!

(Time passes. The baby begins to cry; JEN disappears into the nursery. The crying stops. Pause. HAKIJA enters, and JEN emerges from the bedroom, freshly showered, her hair wet; she takes particular care to close the door all the way behind her; we hear it click under:)

    HAKIJA. Hey.
    JEN. Welcome home.

(They kiss. During the following, he is oblivious to JEN'S manner.)

    HAKIJA. How was your day?
    JEN. How was yours is the question?
    HAKIJA. Oh, he's incredibly nice.
    JEN. Bob?

    HAKIJA. He really is. Very shy, sort of, sly – he has this smile that creeps up, I think to let you know that he's not an asshole or going to demand center stage --

HAKIJA. You want a glass?

JEN. Sure.

HAKIJA. I really liked him, and the scene, I don't know, we'll see.

JEN. Thank you. Tchin tchin.

HAKIJA. Tchin tchin. Oh god, it was just, well, I mean, at the same time that I was thinking, you know, I can handle this, I've earned this, I've gotten myself here, nobody else has, I mean, we have, gotten ourselves here, but... it's not like, I don't know, I had to keep going, don't, you know, just play the scene, and then at the same time I couldn't, oh, it was crazy. You okay?

JEN. What else?

HAKIJA. He played off everything I gave him, he was very open, not bossy. At all. Almost, I don't know, it was fun. So. *(Notices the videotape.)* What's this?

JEN. Came for you.

HAKIJA. What is it?

JEN. I haven't looked.

HAKIJA. Who sent it?

JEN. Put it in the machine.

HAKIJA. All right. You seem ...

(HAKIJA looks at the tape, inserts the tape into the VCR, turns on the TV. Hold, static, then the tape comes on -- we do not see the screen. There is the laughter of men, then the sound of a woman begging in Serbo-Croatian, and the laughter grows more raucous. The woman screams, petrified. HAKIJA turns off the tape.)

HAKIJA. Where did you get that?

JEN. It was a gift.

HAKIJA. I see.

(Silence.)

HAKIJA. There was no choice for us. When the Serbs came through, it was clear that we either participated or we were killed. I know this is very difficult for you to believe or to understand. Miloseviç opened the prisons and made an army out of criminals, the most deranged and violent criminals he could find. They drove all the efforts. One was either one of them or one was dead, those were the two choices. *(Silence.)* There isn't anything ...*(Silence.)* You have no way of imagining. It was worse than a nightmare. I know ... you see me on the tape, but that's, if I didn't ... if we didn't all play along ... There were only two choices. You think I'm proud of ... Christ oh Christ. *(Pause.)* Is Naomi sleeping? *(Silence.)* Please, Jen. What do you want me ... ? The war was ending ... I took his passport, I hadn't killed him, but ... I could have; it could have been anyone. We were, yes, I'd grown up with him; I had my picture attached to it; it wasn't difficult. I didn't want to be that man anymore. I promise you that I did not ... choose ...

(HAKIJA rises moves to the bedroom door, tries it; it is locked.)

HAKIJA. ... What did you do? *(He jiggles the lock harder.)* Where's the key? Do you have it?

(He throws his weight against the door; it does not budge; it hurls himself against it several times:)

HAKIJA. Naomi. Come on! Naomi!

(He continues kicking it, slowly loosening the hinges, the lock and with one final, violent kick, the door opens, and HAKIJA rushes in.)

HAKIJA. *(From off.)* Where is she? *(Returns)* What have you done with her?

(JEN picks up the phone and dials, waits a second.)

HAKIJA. What are you doing, where's Naomi? Please, Jen, please god –
    JEN. Come on over.

(She hangs up, opens the front door.)

HAKIJA. Who is that? Don't torture me like this, I'll do whatever you want –

(NATHANIEL walks in with the baby in his arms.)

NATHANIEL. Shh, I just got her to sleep, took forever. What's the matter? Should I ... ?
    JEN. Stay. Here.
    NATHANIEL. What happened?
    JEN. Ask him.
    NATHANIEL. Did someone die?
    JEN. Yes. Tell him. Tell him who died. I wanted you to know what it is like to lose a daughter. To not know where she was or what had happened to her, to fear the worst, if only for a few seconds.
    HAKIJA. Thank you.
    NATHANIEL. What happened?
    JEN. We'll tell you. In time.
    HAKIJA. Oh, thank you. Oh my god ... I'm sorry, I'm

sorry, thank you ...

NATHANIEL. Jen?

JEN. "Time, the all-seeing, has found us out against our will."

HAKIJA. I'm so sorry ... Thank you ...

JEN. *(To us.)* I knew what was on the tape without watching it. "Why should any man fear the gods if chance is all there is? Better to live one's life without fear [...] Those who give it no more thought than that are the happiest." I remember that. I forget the rest. I don't believe in tragedy. Did you know that there is no other word for it in any other language, it is always a variant of the Greek word: tragedy. It belongs to them ... I choose to be happy. To me Oedipus is a fool. I don't cry for him, I cringe. Jocasta, on the other hand, all she's trying to do is protect her marriage – her first by murdering the child who threatens it, and her second by hiding the truth from her husband, once she knows. I don't want to be Medea. I choose to be happy. You can do that. You really can. Hak still always says that Americans don't understand tragedy, and I hope that could always be true. Don't you? Well ... God bless you. May He keep us all from harm. Goodnight.

(End of play.)

APPENDIX* (continuing the conversation on page 68 after Nathaniel's line "That's actually the one way … ")

NATHANIEL. *(Sound lowered on.)* If you were going, I were going to take a particular, you know, slant on the play – I mean, that would be the one I'd – and I'm not going to do that, I hate that in productions where you can see the goddamn point of view of the director like handprints from a blind person feeling their way around the set after they've fallen into paint: you see?, it's all about the "Riddle of Human Identity" – who are we? It's all about repression, right????, and the Freudians all leap up and cheer, or it's about rootlessness, the homeless! Oedipus, poor thing, is thrust out of his warm home as an infant no less and then he's thrust out again, for good, and blind no less, as an adult! Social workers, take note. And socialists. Or it's about the civilized versus the bestial, our cultural, learned behavior in opposition to the savage creature within who must then be cast out, the scapegoat, you see! Tragedy itself, the word, is based on this: the goat! Goat festival, or some fucking thing, Paola can tell you. OR OR it's about pollution, inside and out, OR as some, one of us suggested Oedipus is Athens, read "America," get it?!?, or it's about the search for ultimate meaning, is suffering what gives us meaning or is it the search for meaning that causes us to suffer so much?!? OR, is it all some juridical debate as to which laws are still appropriate – all the ACLU-ers would line up around the block. That shit is easy! Oh, wow, he's saying is it a random universe or do the gods have a plan, no matter how inscrutable! You'd win an Obie for that. And and … I don't know … I'm …

FANNY. No, I'm listening.

NATHANIEL. I've finished grinding my ax.

FANNY. I sort of see what you're saying.

NATHANIEL. That's just me, you know.

* At some point during this, Fanny responds to the conversation between Paola and Christmas about the women he's slept with. If it interrupts the above scene, then she returns to Nathaniel with a contrite expression, and he will have held, patiently, for her return.

APPENDIX B (Oedipus, Shepherd, Messenger.) – Insert Begins on page 8

OEDIPUS. You! Ancient fellow, look me straight in the eye. Did you ever belong to King Laius?

SHEPHERD. I did – born and raised in the palace, not purchased on the block.

OEDIPUS. What were your tasks?

SHEPHERD. Herding, all my life.

OEDIPUS. Where? I didn't ask how long.

SHEPHERD. Cithaeron, the foothills.

OEDIPUS. Ever seen this man before?

SHEPHERD. No, I … Wait … my memory's going …

MESSENGER. So many years we worked together, you don't remember me at all?

SHEPHERD. Maybe I do, don't rush me, everything was long ago.

MESSENGER. You don't remember giving me an infant to raise?

SHEPHERD. Shh, why dredge that up now?

MESSENGER. Here he is – look!

SHEPHERD. Shut your mouth, you need a thrashing!

OEDIPUS. You need the lash more than he, old fool.

SHEPHERD. Your majesty, what … ?

OEDIPUS. Answer his question!

SHEPHERD. Don't torment an old man, I'm begging you.

OEDIPUS. Twist his arm – Hard!

SHEPHERD. No – God help me –

OEDIPUS. Did you give him a child?

SHEPHERD. I wish I'd died … instead …

OEDIPUS. You did?

SHEPHERD. The more I say, the more you'll torture me!

OEDIPUS. *(To the Messenger.)* Harder! More!

SHEPHERD. Yes! YES! I did.

OEDIPUS. Where did you get this child?

SHEPHERD. No more – I can't remember—

OEDIPUS. Break his arm in two.

SHEPHERD. From the palace!

OEDIPUS. Slave or royalty?

SHEPHERD. I can't.

OEDIPUS. Cut him open!

SHEPHERD. It was his own son, Laius!

OEDIPUS. My wife? Gave you this wretched child?

SHEPHERD. Yes, my lord. To kill. I was to slay the babe.

OEDIPUS. Her own?

SHEPHERD. Yes! Yes. To foil the prophecy.

OEDIPUS. And you disobeyed? You dared to … ?

SHEPHERD. I am lost!

OEDIPUS. Lost! I'm lost – Exposed. Cursed at birth, cursed in wedding, cursed in murder.

JUMP / CUT
Neena Beber

Winner of the L. Arnold Weissberger Award

Three bright urbanites want to make their mark on the world. Paul is a hardworking film-maker on the rise. His girlfriend Karen, a grad student, must get on with her thesis or find a life outside of academia. Dave, a life-long buddy whose brilliance is being consumed by increasingly severe episodes of manic-depression, is camping on Paul's couch. Paul and Karen decide to turn Paul into a documentary. The camera is on 24 hours a day, capturing up-close images of his jags and torpors and their responses. How far will love, friendship and ambition take this hip trio? "A remarkable, absorbing, complex and intelligent play."—*Variety*. 2 m., 1 f. (#12918)

STRANGER
Craig Lucas

Strangers on a transcontinental flight gradually reveal things they have never spoken about before: Linda is traveling with a great deal of cash as well as enough pills to kill herself; Hush has just been released from prison after serving fifteen years for kidnapping a young girl and keeping her alive inside a trunk for over a year. An alliance grows based on the shocking aspects of their personal histories. Together they go to a crude cabin in the middle of nowhere where they learn things about themselves and each other that change their lives irrevocably. A mystery, a tragedy, a love story, a requiem and a jaw-dropping shocker, *Stranger* is not suitable for bedtime reading. 2 m., 2 f. (#21446)

For more captivating dramas with small casts, see
THE BASIC CATALOGUE OF PLAYS AND MUSICALS
online at www.samuelfrench.com

THE GENERAL FROM AMERICA
Richard Nelson

The Tony award-winning playwright of *James Joyce's The Dead* draws a captivating, iconoclastic portrait of America's quintessential traitor, Benedict Arnold. The focus is on how and why a military hero who nearly gave his life for the cause of American freedom disclosed vital information to the British. First produced by the Royal Shakespeare Company and in Houston and New York by The Alley Theatre, this is a rewarding look at intrigue in American history. "Takes a Shakespearean approach to Arnold's character.... It exposes the puritanical hypocrisy and corruption that marched beside the heralded courage of our national beginnings."—*Village Voice.* 11 m., 3 f. (#8995)

JUDGMENT AT NUREMBERG
Abby Mann

Maximilian Schell and George Grizzard starred on Broadway in this powerful stage version of the Academy Award-winning film. Issues at the forefront of this trial reverberate through history and challenge humanity to this day. "A powerful work of art."—*AP.* "Gives oratory the muscle, sweat and high stakes of a last man standing prize fight."—*The New York Times.* "Retains its power to move and provoke us."—*Time.* "A powerhouse."—*Newsday.* "Gripping edge-of-the-seat drama."—Walter Cronkite. "Incisive, blistering, thought-provoking.... Crises out powerfully to our own time in countless ways."—*Chicago Sun-Times.* 15 m., 4 f. (#12919)

For the best in historical and courtroom dramas, see
THE BASIC CATALOGUE OF PLAYS AND MUSICALS
online at www.samuelfrench.com

GOOD BOYS
Jane Martin

A fierce encounter between fathers, one black and one white, opens a deeply disturbing chapter in their lives. The men relive the school shooting in which their sons died, one a victim and the other the shooter. When racial issues threaten to derail all hope for understanding and forgiveness, the black father's other son pushes the confrontation to a dangerous and frightening climax. This topical drama by the author of *Keely and Du* and other contemporary hits premiered at the Guthrie Theater. "Galvanizing."—*St. Paul Pioneer*. "A terrifying, terrific piece of theatre that is as memorable as it is unsettling."—*Star Tribune*. (#9935)

THE ANASTASIA TRIALS
IN THE COURT OF WOMEN
Carolyn Gage

This farcical play-within-a-play is an excursion into a world of survivors and abusers. It opens as a feminist theatre group is about to put sisterhood to an iron test: each draws the role she will play on this evening from a hat. The performance that follows is the conspiracy trial of five women accused of denying Anastasia Romanov her identity. The audience votes to overrule or sustain each motion, creating a different play at every performance. "Farce, social history, debate play, agitprop, audience-participation melodrama, satire [that] makes the head reel!"—*San Diego Union-Tribune*. Wild."— *Washington Blade*. 9 f. (#3742)

For comedy and drama for all-male or all-female casts, see
THE BASIC CATALOGUE OF PLAYS AND MUSICALS
online at www.samuelfrench.com